SUNG LITURGY
Toward 2000 A.D.

Virgil C. Funk
Editor

The Pastoral Press

Washington, DC

ISBN: 0-912405-80-5

© 1991 by The Pastoral Press

"Liturgical Reform as Second Reformation" © 1991 by Lawrence
A. Hoffman

The Pastoral Press
225 Sheridan Street, NW
Washington, DC 20011
(202) 723-1254

The Pastoral Press is the publications division of the National
Association of Pastoral Musicians, a membership organization
of musicians and clergy dedicated to fostering the art of musical
liturgy.

Printed in the United States of America

Contents

Preface

The changes occurring in the Roman Catholic Church since the Second Vatican Council have been momentous. No less is true of what has been occurring in other churches and religious traditions. If strict adherence to tradition was a hallmark of the past, today's concern is to re-shape tradition, to form a new and living tradition that is both faithful to the past and yet open to the demands of present and future. This has affected both theology and spirituality, both worship and various other forms of religious practice.

The Roman Catholic Church, in particular, has undergone the most extensive liturgical reform in its history. The bishops gathered at Vatican II initiated a ritual revision that has touched the lives of church members throughout the world. And integral to this modification of worship forms has been a radical change in the way music, singing in particular, shapes common prayer. By fits and starts a new repertory was formed to respond to the demands of a vernacular, participatory worship. New music ministries appeared. New skills were needed. New outlooks were required.

To be sure, some hopes remain unfulfilled. The road has not been easy. There has been pain and frustration. But, naysayers to the contrary, the development of a sung liturgy has slowly taken root. And, in the United States it is beginning to incorporate the cultural genius of Hispanics and Afro-Americans.

What will be the developments in liturgy in the years leading to the end of the twentieth century? What social and religious trends will impact upon the way we worship? What will be the nature and shape of our sung liturgy?

Playing the prophet can be dangerous business. And yet the prophet is not unknown in religious history. This volume contains six presentations originally given at various meetings of pastoral musicians in 1990. The contributors, each assuming a different perspective, assess the problems, the challenges, and the changes facing us as we move on toward 2000 A.D. The future, to be sure, is uncertain, and yet it will be shaped by us.

Virgil C. Funk

1

Liturgical Reform as Second Reformation

Lawrence A. Hoffman

Regular worshipers looking back on the last quarter of a century cannot help but be amazed at the amount of change they have lived through—not only within the Catholic Church (where the reforms of Vatican II are particularly impressive), but in Protestantism and Judaism as well. The following collection of headlines, some of them garnered from actual news clippings, others admittedly contrived from the news of the day that never got reported, presents some idea of what I mean.

1970, Chicago. A large Methodist church announces that it is removing its organ, throwing out its hymnal, and firing the organist. "From now on," the pastor proclaims, "Sunday morning worship will feature the music of Bob Dylan, accompanied by a folk guitar."

1988, First Episcopal Church, Boston. The bishop arrives as usual to confirm this year's crop of candidates, but there is a difference. This year, the bishop is a woman.

1985, New York. A staid Reform temple that once prided itself on its decorum now features upbeat music, clapping, and swaying from side to side. The rabbi says: "It's hard to get people to change, but we're working at it." These Jewish worshipers don't know it, but their music has been influenced by what goes on in uptown Harlem, where the rabbi goes occasionally for an exchange of pulpits. Word has it that, once upon a time, some congregants leaving the black church were heard saying to their rabbi, "Now, that's worship!"

1974, Chicago. The same large Methodist church announces that it is reinstalling its organ, taking another look at the old hymnal, contracting with a new organist, and firing the kid who plays only Bob Dylan.

In 1761 soon-to-be-president of Yale University, Ezra Stiles, looked back on the first Great Awakening and pronounced it a time when multitudes of people were "seriously, soberly, and solemnly out of their wits." Happily for President Stiles, he was not around to witness the next headline. 1981, New Haven. The assistant chaplain at Yale University preaches this Sunday morning at the university's old and prestigious church. This year, the chaplain is not only a woman, but a rabbi as well.

The most significant story, however, is dated 1976. The National Association of Evangelicals announces that it has fifteen million adherents. Added together with those of the American Council of Christian Churches, and those Christians who are confessional conservatives in other church bodies, the total reaches some sixty-million worshipers. In other words, the largest "church" in our country today is evangelical.

The steady increase in evangelical, fundamentalist, and pentecostal religion is readily visible: Billy Graham's crusades are televised nation-wide; Pat Robertson runs for president; a southern Baptist leader publicly doubts that God hears the prayers of the Jews. On the Jewish side of things too, the rise of the right is abundantly evident, again, in part because of its characteristic visibility. From a parked van known as a *Mitzvah-mobile*, Chasidic Jews emerge into midtown Manhattan streets to accost "lapsed" Jews they encounter: "Are you Jewish? Do a *mitzvah* (a religious obligation); put on these *tefillin*" (phylacteries—small boxes containing biblical citations, attached to leather thongs that are wrapped around the arm and forehead, in Orthodox Jewish daily prayers). Right-wing religion looks like news to the press, which finds in it obvious coverage, including background stories on slow days. The image of four thousand Chasidic Jews dressed in black hats and coats praying loudly in the streets of Brooklyn at their leader's birthday party is colorful and, therefore, news. Four thousand liberal Jews in a convention hall and worshiping with texts that have recently been rendered gender inclusive is practically invisible to the cameras and, therefore, not news at all.

The rise in evangelicalism should therefore be seen alongside the less obvious revolution in the liturgical tradition of the "mainline" churches and synagogues in America. This latter development, which includes Jews as well as Christians, is what I mean by a "second reformation." The first reformation was divisive, splitting the western world's Christian community into more and more competing churches. Medieval Jews escaped its effects then, only because a wall of rising anti-Jewish sentiment insulated them from the intellectual challenges which Luther, Calvin, and others raised. By the nineteenth century, however, the reformation reached the growing ranks of emancipated Jews, largely in Germany, where it wrought changes reminiscent of its path through Christian society three centuries earlier. It sliced up the pre-modern but largely unified rabbinic communities into "Reform" and "Orthodoxy." Expanding the notion of "reformation" to Judaism as well as to Christianity is no mere slight of hand. Both groups even developed their own respective counter-reformations, Tridentine Catholicism and Orthodox Judaism, both being instances of the closing of ranks against reformation encroachment. "It is enough for the council that it condemns heresies," announced a sixteenth-century papal legate who knew that if Trent could not decide all theological questions of the day, it could at least stem the tide of change by declaring unauthorized change itself to be heretical. Similarly, the staunchly reactionary nineteenth-century Hungarian rabbi, Moses Sofer, is best known for his aphoristic warning, "Change is in and of itself forbidden by the Torah."

The second reformation through which we are living is quite different from the first. The first reformation divided church and synagogue into warring factions; the second reformation unites those factions back into their respective larger wholes. Denominational separatism is not at stake, but denominational identity is. This is to say, individual churches and sects are no longer separate enclaves, hermetically sealed off from one another. One is still a Methodist, a Reform Jew, or a Catholic, but Methodists marry Baptists and end up as Presbyterians, for instance. More to the point is the cleavage between reformation and counter-reformation forces, in that reformation Catholics, Jews, and Proestants of all confessions have more in common with each other than with counter-reformation forces in their own denominations. The thinking of the first reformation celebrated the specificity of denominational identity, whereas the thought of the second reformation champions that unity and binds churches to each other, and even perceives Jews and Christians as members of a common Jewish-Christian tradition.

When people perceive their identity changing, they change their worship. Thus, the first reformation was defined not solely by its official theologies, but by its liturgical practices. Lutheranism, for instance, is unthinkable without Luther's hymns. What reflects Calvinism better than Calvin's opening liturgical confession reminding all assembled of their utter "depravity"? The Church of England is hard to imagine without its *Book of Common Prayer*. The very first Jewish reforms were such things as adding a choir and a sermon in the vernacular, and pruning the old prayer book (now translated from the Hebrew) of its theologically intolerable presuppositions. The second reformation too is worship-centered: new prayer books, hymnals, music and worship styles, to which we shall return at the end of this study.

Finally, what Europe was to the first reformation, America is to the second. Not that this reformation is limited to America's borders. The global village in which we live is hardly amenable to narrow nation-state thinking any more. But it is an American phenomenon, in the sense that the American spirit peremates the changes through which we are living. To study the liturgical revolution in our time is largely to study American religiosity coming of age.

It is convenient to divide American religious history into four discrete stages: *colonization, consolidation, camouflage,* and finally, a genuine American *calling*. A glance at each of them in turn will clarify the reasons for seeing our current reformation as something American in essence; at the same time, it will provide some perspective on the exciting era through which we are now living.

COLONIZATION

It is commonplace to describe America as the history of immigrants and colonists. Such a view is only partly true, of course, since by the time European immigrants arrived, Native Americans had already been here for centuries. African Americans, moreover, arrived not as colonists at all, but as slaves. Still, the majority who did come to colonize America set their stamp upon it firmly and absolutely, so that they are responsible for what transpired here, whether we like what happened or not. And in that sense, our earliest history as a nation is a period of colonization, since the colonists established American culture, for good and for evil.

The very first colonists were the Puritans, who came here, as the saying goes, "for religious freedom"—more properly, their own religious freedom. They outlawed Anglicans and expelled Anne Hutchinson to Rhode Island. For their part, Anglicans in Virginia chased Puritans and Catholics up to Maryland and passed laws banning Baptists and Quakers.

By the nineteenth century, ethnicity began greatly to compound religious divisiveness. German Pietists, already here in large numbers, were joined by Germans of all sorts: Protestants mostly, but Catholics and Jews as well. The extent of the ethnic migrations can be gauged from the case of the Irish. In 1845, the year of the potato blight, already one million Irish Catholics were here. Soon that number would double. By 1851, two million more Irish had either died or moved as a result of the famine back home. That classic period of immigration ended only with the Johnson-Reed legislation of 1921 and 1924, but not before the religious and ethnic landscape of America had been transformed far beyond what anyone could possibly have imagined a century before.

The new waves of immigration did not bring any new sense of religious tolerance; if anything, it aggrevated the biases already present, since now religious intolerance across denominational lines was compounded by equal prejudice rooted in national origins. German Catholics could now fight Irish Catholics, for example as in the following case taken from the archdiocese of St. Paul in which German Benedictines had established an abbey. Archbishop Ireland of St. Paul decided it was unseemly for the good monks at Collegeville to be drinking so much beer at every meal. He suggested it might be a good idea to ban it, to which Abbot Wimmer is reported to have responded: "Even the Trappists don't drink water!"

On the not-so-light side, the Jewish camp featured ideological battles between German Jews who had arrived in mid-century, and eastern European Jews who came in much larger numbers at the century's end. Within the Orthodox camp, Germans looked down at Russians and Poles, just as they had in Europe, while the easterners spoke disparagingly of German arrogance. Non-Orthodox Jews split denominationally along ethnic lines. Reform Judaism here was a German product, the pride of the upwardly mobile Jewish upper class, such as New York's fashionable "Our Crowd." Polish Jews gravitated elsewhere, eventually forming the constituency of America's newly formed Conservative Movement, which operated out of a seminary financed and built by Germans who wanted their newly arrived poor cousins with their outlandish ways to become Americanized, but not necessarily to sit beside them in the same pews.

The Protestants, already splintered into many denominations, merely added more, and fought—sometimes literally— for an increasing market share of the available souls. As the South and the West were "won," Methodists, Baptists, Disciples, and Presbyterians acted as if they had squatter's rights, not on the territory, but on the religion of settlers, who were only waiting to be missionized. The old Puritan stock, led now by Yale's Timothy Dwight, reacted to "losing" the Midwest, the West, and the South, by allocating some of the old New England money to launch missionaries to Hawaii (then the Sandwich Islands). Dwight dreamed aloud of the day when, as he put it, "not one Romish cathedral will still stand."

Religious distrust amounting at times to violent antipathy was the norm. The Mormons were hounded from New York to Missouri to Illinois to Salt Lake City. And even the black Methodists failed to agree on a single church, so that almost overnight the AME and the AME Zion were formed, one in Philadelphia and the other in New York, because their leaders, at least, differed on what their minority faith should be.

So despite the growth in separate churches as guaranteed by law, there was no pluralism, for the simple reason that we were still too European oriented. The map of our world was our familiar Mercator projection, with Europe in the center, and the center of the center, so to speak, zero degrees longitude, running right through England, the chief colonial power. On England's map, Asia did not exist, except around the fringes, and Africa was colored according to the European countries that owned it—primarily Great Britain, whose vast empire on which the sun never sat was iconographically displayed by ubiquitous red splotches all over the page.

This mentality of European religious imperialism transplated in the new world allowed for only two kinds of people: not men and women, or even white and black, but "missionizers" and "missionizees"; and our Euro-centeredness increased as the nineteenth century drew to its close. America's love affair with frontier revivalism reappeared cyclically, but tapered off in the "mainline" churches which decided not to cut their ties to the home church across the ocean, where, it was assumed, "real" religion with roots, existed.

Churches thus sought valiantly to recover their European roots, often demanding a European education of anyone seeking upward mobility in the hierarchy. Roman Catholics, for instance, went to Rome or Louvain. Episcopalians looked, at least, to England for guidance—in New York's General Theological Seminary virtually all of England's Tractarian theology was borrowed, thus tilting American Episcopalianism toward ritualism and the Roman Church. Similarly, Dutch Reformed people looked to Holland; Lutherans looked to Germany or to whatever Scandinavian country they had come from. As late as 1900, ninety-seven percent of the Lutheran Midwest Synodical Conference still used German or another European language for worship.

Even Jews and African Americans, whose situations were unique, shared the late century's yearning for true religion abroad. German Jews found themselves in precisely the same position as German Protestants and Catholics; they too had come to these shores not primarily to escape persecution, but to capitalize on economic opportunity. To be sure, modern anti-Semitism was coming into being in Vienna, Berlin, and other Germanic centers, but German Jews never abandoned the hope that they were witnessing the death pangs of medieval intolerance. They had followed the abortive 1848 revolution with care, but even as the situation worsened at the century's end, the intelligentsia, anyway, retained German as their language of preference, and German culture as a proper antidote for American Philistinism. When World War I broke out, one faculty member of the Hebrew Union College, Gotthardt Deutsch, was so shocked to find Germany opposing America, that he suffered something of a nervous breakdown and stopped attending worship in the chapel. As late as 1969, my German-born Ph.D. advisor told me, only half in jest, that I had better master the "holy tongue," meaning German, not Hebrew, since virtually all serious scholarship prior to World War II was in German.

Conservative and Orthodox Jews hailed largely from the Eastern European countries which had virtually expelled them, following the Czar's infamous 1881 May laws restricting Jewish freedom there. Unlike German Jews, they could hardly imagine themselves going back to Lemberg, Vilna, or Kiev. Nonetheless, they established the fiction that only in the famous European seminaries does real learning take place. On the premise that "real" religion is Eastern European religion, Chasidic Jews to this day dress as they did in eighteenth-century Minsk or Kishinev, as if nothing has changed in two hundred years. After World War II, the famed academy of Telz was transplanted from Poland to Cleveland, but it was not renamed "The Cleveland Academy." If one could not return to Europe, apparently Europe could be transplanted here. The famous Telz Academy thus lives on, but in Cleveland.

The African-American experience was different still. Even before the Civil War, black churches had formed; after the official services to which their owners took them, slaves gathered in brush arbors, where they developed their own unique worship style, replete with "spirituals," which some take to be coded songs of the freedom they sought. The post-war black churches could hardly aspire to "return" to a Europe they had never known, but they too felt the need to look back home for real religious identity. Thus the 1890s witnessed a "back-to-Africa" movement under Bishop Henry McNeill Turner.

In sum, even two or three generations after they arrived, immigrants here were merely a branch office with homes abroad, which informed them how they should be packaged in the American outpost. Simultaneously, the only Americans without a European heritage—Native Americans and African Americans—

were passed over as irrelevant. Even though we had broken free politically in 1776, culturally we were still an appendage of the body that was Europe.

Even those churches that were genuinely Americanized, like the American Baptists and the Methodists, or even the Disciples— an American religious phenomenon *par excellence*—instituted Europe's patterns of religious triumphalism and rivalry. We replicated on these shores Europe's normative state of religious dissension, instituting here a mindset dominated by religious, national, and ethnic wars. Protestants despised Catholics; Catholics erected independent institutions as protection against Protestants; and Jews and Christians met only when necessary. Blacks were invisible, and women were utterly excluded in an era of exclusion generally, an era of private clubs, quotas in colleges, and, eventually, the immigration acts designed to keep out the despised Southern and Eastern Europeans, who by and large, after all, were Catholic and Jewish. White male businessmen ran boards of churches and synagogues the way they did those of corporations like U.S. Steel or Harvard University. Pluralistic we were not; we were a colony, mentally speaking, of old-world European attitudes.

CONSOLIDATION

There was, however, another side to America, the Enlightenment as viewed by those who founded our country, such as Madison and Jefferson, for whom European religious tradition was chiefly a hindrance. The original draft of the Declaration of Independence read: "We hold these truths to be sacred." But that sounded too "churchy" to Franklin or Jefferson, so at the last minute, it was changed to "self-evident."

Thanks to the Enlightenment, religious pluralism grew bit by bit despite the old-world attitudes, so that each phalanx of arriving humanity overlaid its European religious heritage with institutional structures that were compatible with the American enlightenment dream, which is to say, with genuine pluralism. More than any single thinker and actor, James Madison should receive credit for this grand American experiment with religious freedom. In part, Madison believed in a democracy where competing interest groups would prevent any single despotism from arising. In part, though a baptized Anglican and a graduate of Princeton, Madison honestly appreciated the Enlightenment religion of deism at best, even atheism if it came to that. When Virginia threatened to allocate public revenue to churches, albeit allowing individuals to designate which church their funds would support, Madison successfully opposed the measure.

The story from then to now has been the steady socialization of one immigrant group after another, who learn to temper old-world religious intolerance with American pluralism. The process by which American denominations institutionalize Madisonian openness to the religion of others, thus adopting the pluralistic bias of Enlightenment thought, is what I mean by the second stage, American consolidation.

Several factors at the turn of this century hastened the process of American consolidation. Above all, the move to the cities was critical. In 1923 the census declared us no longer a rural phenomenon but an urban one. It was hard to leave the homestead in Iowa, for instance, and come to Chicago. But it was liberating too. It put Americans of all stamps side by side in neighborhoods and assembly lines. Eddie Cantor was singing: "How ya gonna keep 'em down on the farm, after they've seen Paree?" by which we meant New York, not Paris. Urbanization occurred in Europe too, but unlike Europe, American ideology saw pluralism as good, not evil. Revolutions in Europe were viewed as an anomaly, to be followed by reactionary periods that reestablished the *status quo ante*. But the American revolution was intended to be lasting. The economy cooperated as well. Precisely as immigration ceased, the people already here were working their way out of the slums of first-generation squalor, and taking advantage of the opportunities of the Roaring '20s. And finally, ordinary Americans, who seemed to intuit the breakdown of old European antagonisms, flocked in droves to watch baseball games at Comiskey Park or Ebbets Field, where they shared hot dogs and cheers with the people sitting next to them, without asking first what country they came from, or what religion they espoused.

There were exceptions, however. Roman Catholics lagged behind Protestants and Jews, for instance. In the 1890s, the Vatican's support for Americanization culminated in the establishment of

The Catholic University of America, under the guidance of the very progressive John J. Keane. But Leo XIII waffled, at first approving the Americanists, then opposing too much change, and finally, in an encyclical of 1985 (*Longinqua Oceani*), virtually ending the modernist movement. Traditional anti-Catholic bias among Protestants would have hindered general acceptance of Catholicism here in any event. (In 1960, John Kennedy still had to convince Americans that he would not be ruled by the pope, should he be elected president.) But for Catholics, separatism further retarded American consolidation, which was not to come for over half a century.

A second group that was kept out of the pluralistic mix was the black community. The Civil War may have ended official slavery, but it did not guarantee that newly freed black people could claim a right actually to join the American mix. Most denominations of the Reconstructionist era retained parallel black and white churches. Not till 1954, with the Brown vs. Board of Education decision, was "separate but equal" declared to be separate but not so equal; the Civil Rights Act was even then over a decade away; and full integration is still more theory than fact in American culture.

Women too lacked equality here, though their situation was unique, in that they were not envisioned as a distinct group in their own right. Black women were seen as blacks, Catholic women were viewed as Catholics, and so on. The most interesting case study is the women descended from or married into the Protestant establishment. Though excluded from real power, they were granted their own hierarchical system, "separate but equal" to that of the men. They were kept out of the men's clubs, for example, but they had their own status system as Daughters of the American Revolution, or as wealthy patrons of New York's art museums. Their upward mobility frequently entailed charity work, where they established their own pecking order. Between 1910 and 1920, however, growing industrial slums peopled by Europe's newest immigrants began to pose problems beyond the capacity of any volunteer corps to handle, with the result that the women were virtually displaced by government agencies. Turning inward to their own churches, these women began to use their talents as women's auxiliaries. Upper class Jews mirrored the Protestant case precisely. The men banded together to establish such institutions as Chicago's Standard Club or New York's Harmony Club, while their wives worked in settlement houses Americanizing Eastern European immigrants. When the government stepped into the settlement work, the women organized sisterhoods in their respective synagogues.

Two processes were thus at work simultaneously: colonialism as each new wave of immigrants arrived, and consolidation as the wave before it adopted the American pluralistic vision. We were far from absolute equality to be sure, what with the ubiquitous hierarchies ranged along religious, ethnic, gender, and racial lines. But we were equally far from the old-world religious and ethnic warfare also. At least in democratic America, other groups have the right—Madison would have said "the obligation"—to co-exist, and even to be appreciated as valid religious options or, citing Madison again, as "opinions" to which anyone might with good cause adhere.

On the eve of World War II, however, it was still not clear how things would turn out. Henry Ford was publishing his notoriously anti-Semitic *Deaborn Independent*, and had even disseminated a reprinted edition of *The Protocols of the Elders of Zion*, a scurrilous diatribe blaming the evils in the economic sphere on worldwide Jewish conspirators. The Ku Klux Klan had moved north to the cities. Father Coughlin was fulminating in Detroit; President Coolidge himself had written an article favoring white supremacy.

The war years were therefore crucial to the American search for true identity. Fanned by the ravages of the depression, the conflict between the rival perspectives, here labelled colonialism and consolidation, had grown rather than dissipated. But World War II effectively unified Americans as never before. Even then, there were scapegoats, Japanese Americans, this time, who were incarcerated against their will and their rights. But otherwise, Protestants, Catholics, and Jews (whether initially German, Irish, Italian, Polish, or native New Englander)—everyone, it seemed—marched off to war.

If anything sounded the death knell of old-country colonial attitudes of superiority and intolerance, it was the war. The G.I. Joes returned with their European roots in shambles. The British pound might someday be refinanced, bombed-out Dresden might someday be rebuilt, but the ultimately logical conclusion of the colonial mentality, it turned out, was fascism. At the very least, it became clear that all moral and therefore religious leadership could hardly be assumed to come from Europe. Americans had finally found their own moral mandate: the Enlightenment side of European history which had survived on the other side of the Atlantic, as American democracy, American pluralism, the Americanization finally of European religion.

In many ways the war years served as preview for what was to come only decades later. Civil rights, for example, was more rapidly achieved in the army than in civilian life, for the simple reason that military success required a genuine meritocracy with black and white people fighting side by side. Truman's integration order shortly after the war was a recognition of racial equality that has yet to be realized in American culture at large. Meanwhile, back home, Rosie the Riveter was doing men's work, a phenomenon that would not occur again for forty years or more when, at last, "Men working" signs would have to be altered (here and there at least) to include women as well. If we had moved directly to the '60s or '70s, we might have instantly achieved the era I call the American "calling." But it didn't happen quite that way. There were first the '50s to be surpassed and, as we shall see, the apparently heady post-war era of the '50s was hardly the ideal it is usually painted as. For good reason, it can be seen as the inauguration of the third of our four periods: camouflage.

CAMOUFLAGE

We like to imagine the music of the '50s as "oldies but goodies." We like equally to think of the era itself the same way. After nearly four years of World War II followed almost immediately by war in Korea, the mid to late '50s finally gave us a welcome respite from conflict. Wartime technology freed up for peacetime production, and financial well-being in a nation now unquestionably the economic leader of the world made available refrigerators, freezers, television sets, and automobiles in record numbers. A vast interstate highway system opened up the suburbs. Women who delayed having babies until the war ended joined their younger sisters who had just reached the usual age then for giving birth, and together they gave us the vaunted baby boom era.

Clearly, the surface amenities of life were increasing, and with technological progress went the potential, anyway, for cementing American egalitarianism. For instance, contrast radio with the new medium, television. Radio favored stereotypes because you couldn't see who was talking to you. Thus the black people we got from radio were "Amos 'n' Andy" and Rochester; the Jew was stingy Jack Benny. On television, on the other hand, what you get is what you see, especially in the news—witness the painful nightly television newscasts, over a decade later, showing Americans dying in jungles far away, without which it is likely that the Vietnam War would have lasted much longer than it did. There were—still are—stereotypes on television also, especially on the sitcoms where actors played stereotypical roles, like wacky woman Lucille Ball tricking her husband Ricky. Or take *Father Knows Best*, which demonstrated that, on television anyway, fathers (not mothers?) can solve any problem in half an hour. Apparently, within a decade, problems got worse because it took *The Brady Bunch*, all together, an hour to resolve the very same issues.

But television has generally made a valiant effort to reflect trends also. Contrast the old *Dick Van Dyke Show*, with loyal wife Laura Petrie at Rob's side, and the *Mary Tyler Moore Show*: the same actress, appearing now in the showcase city of Minneapolis and working on her own, but not yet in charge. This was an interim show, presaging women's appearance in board rooms with real power (*L.A. Law*). So even though some stereotypes remained, at least old ones could be quickly broken down by new ones, and in any event, news and live telecasts, at least, increasingly did away with our dependence on actors displaying things as we wanted them to be, instead of the way they really are.

What live telecasts gave us in abundance in the '50s was President Eisenhower, often described as the most popular man in American history. Under Ike we celebrated an eight-year victory bash: his smiling face, beamed into our living room regularly—sometimes nightly, was nothing short of an icon of American success. It was a testimonial also to the continuing religiosity of our nation. Newly baptized as he took the presidency, Ike was himself genuinely religious. He liked to tell us that. "I am the most religious man I know," he once proclaimed. In his administration the phrase "under God" was added to the Pledge of Allegiance. His friend, Billy Graham, was a frequent visitor to the White House.

As the suburbs went up, so too did the requisite churches and synagogues, often built right into the blueprints along with the tract homes, the schools, and the golf course. Americans took to religion as never before without, however, particularly caring what religion they took to. Mostly they signed up with their parents—whatever their parents had been, they would be too— as Will Herbert realized in his classic study, *Protestant, Catholic, Jew*. Football had its Big Ten, and religion had its Big Three.

All was not quiet, however, on the critical front. Eisenhower's most frequently cited comment on American religion had been made in 1954: "This nation," he admonished us, "makes no sense unless it is founded on a deeply-felt religious faith, and I don't care what it is." At its best, his comment could have been Jefferson and Madison talking about the possibility of all Americans following their own religious sentiment—genuine pluralism and mutual respect for religious differences at best. At its worst, it was an invitation to the blandness of civil religion, the judgment that our religious selection has no significance because in the new America, all the ancient religions have been melted down into a common dross—like a golden calf, around which the fat calves of the suburbs might dance in their common search for the good life. Will Herberg from the Jewish camp, Reinhold Niebuhr from the Protestant camp, John Courtney Murray from the Catholic camp, all faulted the Big Three for watering down their religious principles and ignoring their historical specificity. We were building a pale version of our historic faiths in what were just three different versions of American civil religion.

Their blistering critiques were not read by many Americans. Preferring television to theology, we tuned into Dinah Shore who was selling us Chevrolets. She sounded credible; everywhere we looked, we saw the new interstate highway system that made the suburbs possible and Chevrolets desirable. Brushing aside the trenchant remarks of Herberg, Niebuhr, and Murray, we experimented with a new phenomenon, suburban religion, housed in churches and synagogues which, like gas stations, grew up on every corner.

Suburban religion was primarily "suburban," only secondarily "religion." From suburbia father commuted to the city, leaving mother and the baby boom kids behind. Religious institutions discovered two new constituencies: mothers and children. Thus was born "pediatric religion."

Floor plans tell the tale: huge school wings and meeting space, but small sanctuaries, which people did not attend anyhow. *Crestwood Heights*, a sociological study of that era, announced the new (and ersatz) religion of Americans: psychotherapy. Churches virtually abandoned worship in favor of a shopping list of programs for suburbanites seeking solace and service: welcome wagons, book clubs, religious schools, and bazaars sponsered by the women's auxiliary. In the religion of the '50s pastors took up psychology or education as their specialty. Worship, by contrast, received short shrift, hardly being taught in most seminaries. The model for the '50s was nonreligious education.

Above all, this was hardly prophetic religion. At best it was religion for the the sake of comforting the financially comfortable. It was for the likes of the Anderson family (*Father Knows Best*) and the Cleavers (*Dennis the Menace*) whose greatest weekly dilemmas revolved around children rather than adults (typically baby boomers, these), and whose problems rarely went deeper than disappointment about Bud Anderson's not having a date for Saturday night. I call it "camouflage" because from the suburbs, the comfortable, white, middle-class people coated their lives saccharin-pretty and pretended that all was well, as if they had nothing better to do than to listen to Snooky Lansen sing "How Much Is That Doggie in the Window?"—a hit song prior to the rock-and-roll revolution.

It was an illusion; really, all was not well in America. Most people had worries beyond how much to pay for a doggie in the window. America was not all suburbs. As comfortable white people abandoned their urban apartments in search of the good life beyond the city limits, old intersections like Fifth and Vine didn't just fade away like the old soldiers of the war just ended.

The inner city was becoming a ghetto for the underclass; racism was rife as never before; black people filled the inner city only to find that for them, there was no way out. Economic disparity grew, compounded by a new wave of immigrants, the Hispanic Americans. Recall, for example, *West Side Story*, which detailed in music and action what you could expect to see in New York's upper west side, before urban renewal constructed Lincoln Center there.

The reaction to this period of camouflage arrived with a vengeance, not by government fiat, but from the grass roots, a natural consequence of the demography: baby boom infants of the '40s and '50s would become baby-boom college students in the '60s and '70s. The largest cohort of Americans thus reached draft age at precisely the time when their country had embarked on the most unpopular war in its history. Television coverage of the war's brutality evoked anti-war sympathy, and simultaneously, by virtue of the medium itself, made every local demonstration a potentially national event, with the result that campuses from Wisconsin to Berkeley and back east again to Columbia, featured one anti-Vietnam War riot after another. Who can forget the 1969 Democratic National Convention in Chicago, with the sneering Mayor Daley within, and the rampaging crowds being bludgeoned by the police without? The nadir of what was becoming our own second civil war came in 1971 when Ohio State National Guard soldiers shot and killed college students at Kent State.

But student unrest ran a lot deeper than a desire to avoid the draft. This new generation of adults was in revolt against much more than the war. The symbolic significance of the war extended deep into the core of society at large, laying bare the rottenness that the saccharine coating of the '50s had camouflaged. The war exploded the myth of the Eisenhower years that all was well. We were at war again (forget the word "conflict"), with an inequitable draft system, and we were losing. If it wasn't clear already, the war left no doubt that a cultural revolution had occurred since the days the suburbs had opened.

The road from the Eisenhower '50s to the Johnson '70s can be traced musically, from "How Much Is that Doggie in the Window?" to Bill Haley and the Comets, to Elvis Presley, and on and on and on. Every time their parents got used to one thing, the kids upped the ante, moving on to something else. The escalating musical taste symptomized a revolt, above all, against blandness: against the pedestrian pretense that the only things worthy of evoking our excitement were country club dinner-dances and school proms.

High on the list of blandness was suburban religion, which evoked a two-pronged revolt, corresponding to two very deeply rooted characteristics of American Protestantism. Christianity in America was founded by Calvinists for whom predestination was a given. With time, however, two competing trends emerged. On the one hand, there was the experience of personal conversion, fostered by evangelists from George Whitefield (1714-1770) to Charles Grandison Finney (1792-1875) and beyond. On the other hand, there was the prophetic desire to correct the world's evils, evident most clearly in the abolitionists or the Social Gospel movement at the turn of the century. The Vietnam years thus spun off not one revolt but two: a search for inner spirituality, sometimes in the established churches and synagogues, and sometimes outside of them but, in any case, akin to conversion; and a popular revolution against social inequities, the war included. It was the revolution that got all the front page news then—the march on Selma (1965); the riots ("Burn, baby, burn!"); Malcolm X and the Black Panthers as signs of black militancy; and, of course, Vietnam, at which we have already looked.

At the same time, though, there was a parallel phenomenon, unabashedly religious, and readily recognizable as a search for adult spirituality by the kids who had grown up in the suburbs and knew first hand that suburban religion was not very religious. Some left their Judaism and Christianity altogether. The Beatles spoke for them when they bathed in the Ganges in 1968. But the Beatles' action was mild compared to others who virtually invaded America with religious alternatives. During the 1960s two hundred thousand people followed the Maharishi Mahesh Yogi into Transcendental Meditation. Hare Krishna got here in 1965. Timothy Leary urged young people to "turn on" with LSD. Flower children and the Age of Aquarius surrounded us.

Yet the Age-of-Aquarius style of religion was only the most visible sign of a religious revival, and not the most important one. Unannounced in the newspapers, for example, Native Americans were taking steps to rediscover their own faith roots in the land, and to reestablish their own rituals, like the spirit quest and sweat lodges. And above all, there was brewing a massive revolt against the established mainline faiths in their watered-down '50s style. This was the beginning of the loyal opposition, the growth of the neo-evangelicals. Despite the long and complex history of evangelical Protestant Christianity in America, most observers had buried the movement by the 1920s, calling it dead. Yet in the 1960s evangelical Christianity seemed to be taking over.

Reference to evangelicalism requires care. There is no single evangelical church, the way there is a Presbyterian or a Catholic Church. Evangelicalism thus means many things to many people, depending on the context. Here, I differentiate evangelicalism *as a search* for personal conversion, from evangelicalism *as a movement* intent on denying the licit status of non-evangelicals in general within Christianity, and of non-Christian religion in particular. Evangelicalism as a search is perfectly in keeping with the inner life of the spirit common to Christianity and to Judaism, albeit describable in different technical nomenclature—Jews would speak of being a *ba'al teshuvah*, for instance, someone who "has returned" to God. It is also consistent with the pluralistic Madisonian ethic which I describe as the hallmark of American consolidation. *Evangelicalism as a movement*, on the other hand, is particularistic: genuine conversion occurs only in a given Christian context with a given Christian content. Insofar as it opposes religious pluralism, it is more in keeping with the colonizing perspective, where the basic binary opposition is "missionizers" vs. "missionizees."

It is *evangelicalism as a movement*, best symptomized in the unsuccessful, but nonetheless striking, "Key-73" campaign, which is relevant here, in that as much as the liturgical revolution was prompted by the failure of suburban religion, it was given its most immediate goad by the evangelicals who were reacting to the same phenomenon and whose success threatened to destroy the liberal churches. To a great extent, then, the liturgical revival of the "mainstream" can thus be seen as a response to the bland civil religion of the '50s, and to the rise of neo-evangelicalism itself. That is to say, the religious establishments faced two threats, not just one. First, came the religious debacle in which serious religion was leveled to pablum. But more pressing, if anything, was the second threat: evangelicalism (of the non-pluralistic Key-73 variety) which captured the religious imagination of some sixty million alienated Christians by 1976.

Established churches thus took their own steps to transform their spiritual life into a valid religious alternative for adults. In so doing they emphasized precisely those values that their evangelical opponents appeared to deny: inclusion, universalism, and egalitarianism. Implicit too in their re-formulation of the Christian message is a return to prophetic ethics, notoriously missing in the 1950s and shunned (in part) by evangelicals who view it as part of the liberalism that got us into the bind we are in in the first place. The liturgical revolution thus combines a reaction against suburban blandness and evangelical absoluteness. At the same time, it continues both prongs of the earlier revolution of the 1960s: a search for spirituality, and a call for social action.

Every reformation has its counter reformation as well. We can now be clear about the two sides, as they began to emerge from the decade of Vatican II. The reformation cuts across religious lines, as does the opposition to it. In fact, denominational identity is often less crucial than whether one is within the reformation camp or outside of it. The reformation includes all those forces who respond to the '50s by calling for renewed spirituality within established church and synagogue bodies; who further appreciate Madison's thoroughgoing pluralism; who therefore have put aside whatever traditional religious triumphalism they once had, and instead, attempt now to see former religious enemies as licit theological allies and neighbors in a world where every person is both unique and equal; and who, finally, argue for a renewed policy of social justice without which the new liturgies' adult spirituality might be said to be morally flawed because it is selfishly conceived.

The counter-reformation includes both those who wish to return to a pre-Vatican II mentality (or its equivalent in Protestant and Jewish circles) and the evangelical response to the '50s insofar as the response leaves no room for pluralism.The former include the obvious candidates, like Catholicism's *Opus Dei,* and Reform Jews who want to return to the *Union Prayer Book* with its sexist language and old ritual forms that celebrated the arrival of

"Our Crowd" in mainline America. The latter includes the Protestants I meet from time to time who want to convert me, such as a man sitting next to me on a plane recently, who assured me he prays all the time for the Jews to end their blindness. But it includes also Chasidic Jews on the right, Judaism's own evangelical force, who have no desire to evangelize Christians, but who think their Christian equivalents are right about one thing at least (though for the wrong reasons)—the religious blindness of liberal Jews like me.

As I speak of a fourth stage in American religion, the one that prompts liturgical renewal in the historic churches and synagogues, I do so, obviously, not as an objective observer but as a member of the reformation forces. My bias in favor of Madisonian democracy, pluralism, egalitarianism, social justice, and an end to sexism and racism is explicit in my formulation of this essay. What follows is a description of synagogue and church liturgical reform, from the perspective of one who has participated in it, and thinks it a good thing. That I call it an American Calling should surprise no one.

CALLING

Though Vatican II was the cultural symbol of the new age, liturgical reform did not begin there. Within Catholicism itself, many years of the liturgical movement preceded the council and made the council possible in the first place. Still, the changeover to a new stage in American religion is best symptomized, even heralded, by the Catholic reforms. Since the failure of Americanism in the 1890s, the Roman Catholic Church here had been the least acculturated of all church bodies. If Catholics could change, went the feeling, surely others could as well.

The event of Vatican II occurred in Rome, but it was worldwide in its causes and effects. And interestingly enough, the statement on religious pluralism—the Declaration on Religious Freedom (*Dignitatis Humanae*)—was American through and through. It had been drafted by John Courtney Murray, and it was fought through by John Cardinal Ritter of St. Louis and the American bishops, who knew that American pluralism could instruct world Catholicism in its vision of religion.

But what was immediately evident in Catholicism was equally present, if less obviously, in American Protestant and Jewish bodies too. The liturgical renaissance characterizes Catholic, Protestant, and Jew alike. New worship books, music, and styles speak eloquently of the values I have labelled the American calling. What, then, are the challenges of this age of calling, which I call the "new reformation"?

First, we are moving to a period of genuine inclusivity of religious tradition. Liturgy-of-the-word-centered churches have rediscovered the eucharist, while eucharist-centered worshipers are rediscovering the word. Liturgical faiths that have relied only on single, fixed liturgies in books now discover what free-church-style prayer can do, and the free church tradition is beginning to re-evaluate some elements of a written liturgical heritage. Christianity in general has reached out to emphasize the role of religious memory, even memory that stretches back through time to find Christian origins embedded in rabbinic Judaism. And Judaism, for its part, has started to reach out ecumenically to Christians, thus whittling away at the old presumption that "dialogue" is just a stratagem for proselytizing. Both Jews and Christians appear ready to affirm each other's spiritual quest, and even to learn from each other along the way.

We used to define ourselves by what liturgical things we do not do. Now what matters is what we do. We become inclusive, not exclusive. Christians speak more often now about those with whom they are or might be in communion, rather than those who are necessarily outside the liturgical pale. On appropriate occasions—Thanksgiving Day, for instance—Jews and Christians tend increasingly to meet for worship in common. Inclusivity of tradition implies going to our past to recover liturgical models long forgotten; it implies expanding the liturgical canon of what is permitted, allowing for choice among the many licit options we unearth. We thus come up with thick worship books, larger hymnals, optional services, choices of readings, a sense that worship may proceed in ways we have never considered before.

The challenge for each of us is to ask whether we are taking full advantage of the new texts, settings, music, and ideas for worship; or whether our thinking still antedates the new reformation, so that we just go through the same service in the same old way, just as we were used to. Imagine someone inventing the waltz and presenting it to people who know only the march. New worship texts and music "played out" according to old paradigms is tantamount to performing the waltz in old-fashioned march tempo, thus missing the whole point of the new discovery.

Second, we are moving toward inclusivity in our congregations and assemblies. Christian theology that sees the assembly as "the church" is apt here, as is the Jewish insistence on having a quorum (*a minyan*) at prayer, so that the congregation assembled is in fact *am yisra'el*, the people Israel. The influence of the feminist critique has been central in this regard. We are moving toward an age of gender and racial equality, and to an appreciation of what individuals as individuals in our worshiping assemblies bring with them out of their own ethnic or religious past. Catholics, for example, must recognize that not everyone is white and raised in a Roman Catholic Church that harks back to baroque architecture, Bernini art, and the great and glorious music of Trent. At a recent workshop for chaplains, an Episcopalian priest who traced his family all the way back to the seventeenth century complained about today's new hymnals. "What happened to the good old favorites that we don't sing any more?" he wanted to know. A black colleague quickly responded, "They're not my 'old favorites'." A pluralistic community of worshipers will have to make room for cultural idiosyncracy by developing the will to transcend the limitations of the majority's traditional liturgical/theological bill of fare.

We now know that there is a surfeit of authentic traditions out there: churches are challenged to appreciate the Hispanic tradition and gospel music, for instance; synagogues can recover Sefardic chant; all of us can learn to balance the male-derived and designed style of our worship with new forms that bespeak the equal reality of women's experience. The challenge goes beyond just expanding the liturgical "canon," so to speak; the real issue is to accept what an expanded canon signifies: our resolve to welcome people whose alternative traditions we now call our own.

We are challenged to take advantage of the richness of diversity. Do we seek out the prayer experiences of all our members, or are we mired in the pre-reformation consciousness in which there is only one way—the colonialist way—to pray?

Third, we have become genuinely people-centered. The '60s preached "Power to the people"; we now promise "Prayer to the people!" If their worship is not their own, it belongs to no one. The new accent is distinctly on involvement.

We can return worship to worshipers, but ony with a new ecclesiology. Christians will return to the early church model, rather than the medieval one. Jews will adopt the Kabbalistic notion of *tsimtsum*, whereby the prayer leader emulates God in withdrawing from the universe so as to leave room for people to develop themselves.

The challenge, then, is to discover if our worship is affirming of people. Is it prepared by a professional team *for* people, or do the people themselves have a say in the planning? Are worshipers silent, passive, obsequious puppets who are sungat, and preached to, or do they sing together, and move with purpose, alive to the very miracle of being alive?

Finally, there are the twin foci which were to be seen in the revolutions of the '60s: the prophetic demand for social justice, and the search for a genuine adult spirituality. Prophetic faith helps us to see worship as transformative, positing a new world, a social reconstruction of an alternative reality that we intuit in the words of our prayers, the unity of the disparate individuals gathered together in worship, the very style of prayer that affirms each of us as part of a greater whole. We may come to pray, convinced of the sorry state of today's world. But we leave transformed into believers in the happier state of what we, working with God, may bring into being. We read of it in our lectionary, hear it preached from the pulpit, assert it in our prayers, and watch its vision dance in the gaze of those whose eyes we catch as we look about the room. Worship at its best is the surest promise of a better time we name the *eschaton*, *olam haba*, the reign of God, the messianic age.

Worship must affirm religious promise; it must carry over to the worshipers' acting differently in the world. It should be conversionary in the sense that we emerge from worship differently.

Our challenge is to know whether people leave our worship affirmed in their faith to the extent that they act it out in the world, beyond the context of the hour of prayer. Or do they come simply out of obligation, and leave carrying no sense of the prophetic call for justice away with them?

But the prophetic and the spiritual are not mutually exclusive. They go together. So in addition to the focus on a prophetic ethic comes the focus on a rediscovery of God among us. There was a time in European spirituality, carried to these shores, when we knew that God was transcendent; we designed sacred space and outfitted it with music that spoke of grandeur. We were convinced that God was surely in heaven, transcendent and awe-inspiring, calling us only to recognize the overwhelming divine presence of cosmic proportions.

There is still a time and place for that. But there is another side to God, a side named by Christians as the incarnate Jesus Christ, and by Jews as the *shechinah*: this is the God who sits among us, suffers with us, knows us intimately as friend and supporter. Particularly in America, this quiet intimate spirituality finds its place. As American democracy has broken down social distance, it has similarly discovered a God who is not so distant from ordinary people. We are challenged to arrange our worship to celebrate a God among us, not simply a God who looks down on us from the great and glorious distance beyond.

The discovery of God among us, even at moments of divine encounter, implies an expansion of worship beyond the set hours, the official calendar, the three obligatory services for Jews. A final challenge, then, is whether we are using prayer as fully as we might. In our homes? In hospitals and hospices? At ordinary meetings? At moments of personal gratitude? At meals and re-unions? The list is endless.

* * * * * *

If these, our challenges, are not soon met, the reformation will fail. We have pinned our hopes on changes that run deep and are not easily accomplished. Can we, in fact, expand our inherited liturgical canons to be inclusive of all the best that our specific traditions allow? Can we really recast centuries of monolithic certainty to the point that our worship demonstrates reverence for the pluralism of the assembled gathering, and for other gatherings of other faiths as well? Will we manage to return prayer to the people, and to establish the twin primacy of justice and spirituality in a worship that transcends the pediatric pulp of the '50s? Truth be told, there is reason to doubt that we will succeed.

A healthy body of evidence demonstrates that churches and synagogues are no longer the places people go for their spiritual needs. New liturgies are one thing. Restructuring entire institutions is another. That is why the liturgical renewal must be seen as more than something in and of itself. It is, at bottom, part of a larger enterprise: a reformation with which Americans are charged to enter the new century.

[I am much in debt to many people for this essay. The mistakes are my own, of course, but I drew on the supportive data contained in the work of Sidney Ahlstrom, James Davison Hunter, Martin Marty, Jaroslav Pelikan, James F. White, and Robert Wuthnow. I offer them my gratitude.]

2

Facing the Hard Issues

Mary Collins, O.S.B.

Participants in this conference on Liturgy in Dialogue with the World must assume, as did the program framers, that there is a connection between our public worship and our engagement in our national and world culture but that the connection is not yet well-articulated. Here is life in this world. Somewhere nearby is our liturgy. Here is Nelson Mandela leading the struggle against the culture of apartheid; here are city school children trying to play and study in our urban war zones. Here are women trying to balance the many claims on their lives—employment, children, elderly parents, a husband, responsible family planning; here are legislators trying to determine whether there is a peace dividend after all and who has claim upon it. Here are environmentalists telling us we are burying ourselves in plastic waste, disposable diapers, and toxic chemicals; here are the National Rifle Association and the National Endowment for the Arts each interpreting for us our constitutional rights.

Not too far away is our Sunday assembly. Shall we have girls serving at the altar? Shall we have communion in two kinds? Must the lay ministers dress in albs or may they? Shall the extraordinary lay ministers of communion yield their place to the visiting concelebrant or the vacationing seminarian who has been installed as acolyte? Can we get a piano for the folk group? Can we have infant baptisms at Sunday Mass without warning the people, since they are coming for Mass and not for the baptism of some stranger's kid?

Not everyone agrees with the operating assumption that liturgy ought to connect—however tenuously—with life. The countervailing view is that liturgy is timeless, eternal mystery, respite from daily life in this world, a place of refuge for communion with God. But this conference stands in continuity with the great leaders of the nineteenth- and twentieth-century liturgical movements: from Prosper Gueranger to Lambert Beauduin to Pius X to Virgil Michel to Pius XII and from them to the world's bishops assembled in council in 1960s. Their shared view can be summed up in a pair of statements. First, these times call for social regeneration. And second, restoration of the liturgy to greater authenticity is the key to such social regeneration.

Their great claim, boldly held, was only partially articulated, but they pressed it on the church with unwavering conviction. Liturgical reform is the basis for ecclesial renewal; ecclesial renewal will result in social regeneration. Theirs was a benign variant of the domino theory; they had little doubt that one matter would lead inevitably to the next.

Now in 1990 we have new liturgical books signaling a liturgical reform in process; and we have innumerable major and minor skirmishes in parishes and dioceses about Sunday eucharist, the baptism of children, of adults, confession and penance services, confirmation, communion for the sick, and the anointing of the sick. We issue instructions, directories, authentic interpretations for the proper implementation of the liturgical reform.

But we also have AIDS and apartheid, and the disappeared and the drug wars, and teenage pregnancies and clerical pedophilia. So we come to the hard issue: what is happening to this liturgical renewal after all? Among currently available judgments is one reported to me this month, that "liturgical reform was a trick of the devil, " warned against by Our Lady of Fatima, whose warning the popes and bishops ignored, with the result that the church is being destroyed from within. Fortunately, an alternate assessment is available to explain our as-yet-less-than-satisfactory meeting between liturgy and life.

Our Present Situation within the Liturgical Reform

Recall that the first of the intended outcomes of liturgical reform was ecclesial renewal. We anticipated that the Christian people, newly informed by the spirit of the liturgy, would become light to the world, salt of the earth, leaven in the mass of humanity, ambassadors of reconciliation, agents of the dawning reign of God. First a new church, and in its wake a new world.

The liturgical reform program set out in *Sacrosanctum Concilium*, the Vatican II constitution on the liturgy, was envisioned as having two stages. In stage one, reformers would restore the Roman Liturgy to its classic form, as the form has been made known through historical research. We might have imagined the task of stage one either as a pruning project or as a building restoration project. Cut away not only dead wood but even green wood to let the shrub grow again from its solid roots. Or gut the building that has been renovated and redecorated many times for many purposes, so that its current occupants can give it a shape more hospitable for them and more welcoming to strangers. Stage one's achievement was the Roman *editio typica*, the revised liturgical books.

In stage two, we expected to let the local churches in communion with Rome promulgate, translate, celebrate, and then adapt the Roman *editio typica* to their own genius while maintaining their communion with the church at Rome, maintaining "the substantial unity of the Roman rite." This approach to the renewal task was intelligible to liturgical historians at least. The expected outcome would be similar to what happened in an earlier historical moment in the ninth century when the liturgical books of the church of Rome were sent to Charlemagne's liturgists in northern Europe. The churchmen who received them promptly adapted them to meet the pastoral needs and expectations of the Germanic tribes as these needs were interpreted by the emperor and his associates among the clergy. It was cultural adaptation initiated at the top.

After the Second Vatican Council, conferences of bishops were designated to preside over such adaptations of the Roman liturgical books as they judge necessary for the genius of their churches, and then to get confirmation of their actions from the Roman See (Constitution on the Sacred Liturgy, nos. 37-40). The reform program was based on the presumably unconscious and certainly unexamined premise that a past experience of liturgical development could be replicated under controlled conditions in this present moment. Subsequently the expectation about a smooth, centrally directed, transformation of liturgical rites has been recognized as naive in its innocence, lacking awareness of the most rudimentary social analysis and social theory. But even if a replication of reform under controlled conditions had been theoretically possible, the two-stage plan was neither well-understood nor well-supported, even by those to whom it was entrusted.

It was not well-understood. Some (most?) members of episcopal conferences and diocesan presbyterates presumed stage one was "it;" that is, the *editio typica* Roman books were themselves the intended outcome of the reform. We got new books and we translated them into the vernacular, but we used them very much as we had used the old books. Acclamations like triple "alleluias" were as likely to be recited as to be sung. Or we used the new liturgical books selectively, preferring the parts familiar from the old books. So the provision for communion under both kinds was perceived to be an option, not an integral part of a full eucharistic celebration. So also the specification that the bread for the eucharist should look like bread and be fractioned ritually for distribution was commonly seen as precious rather than as pastorally necessary.

Some worshipers, including the ordained, gave the new liturgical books bad reviews, calling them "boring," "wordy," "unimaginative," "unexciting," because they mistook the books for the performance by a fully engaged assembly. The stark texts of the new vernacular liturgy have encouraged some older Catholics to indulge in nostalgia for the "mystery" of the good old days and to lure a new post-conciliar generation into a pseudo-nostalgia for something they called "tradition."

If the reform was not well-understood, neither was it well-supported. Under these conditions, stage two of the liturgical reform was fated to be stillborn. The production of books in stage one had been entrusted to special bodies of liturgical experts. And when their task of producing the Roman *editio typica* was completed, many went back to their research institutes and universities with confidence that in due time episcopal conferences all over the world would act to initiate stage two. The national episcopal conferences of India and of Zaire took the expected initiatives early. But with the post-conciliar book-producing task forces dispersed, with all the experts dedicated to renewal having gone home, the responsibility for facilitating stage two reverted to the Roman Curia.

It is no secret that many of our brothers in that Roman body had no commitment to the project; they embraced neither the basic reform of the ritual books nor what the constitution called cultural adaptation. Many in fact had a genuine dislike for the very premises of the project. And they have acted effectively in the past decade to turn procedures on their head. It was the expectation of the framers of *Sacrosanctum Concilium* that their brothers in service to the Roman See would receive and confirm the adaptations of the Roman liturgy that episcopal conferences around the world judged to be authentic expressions of paschal-faith in their local churches. But many Roman curial secretaries and congregational prefects began in the decade of the 1980s to judge as unreliable the judgments of national and regional epis-copal conferences. Worse yet, many bishops and conferences of bishops have come to accept this reversal of procedures as not only acceptable but inevitable.

Naming the Present Situation

Thus, in decade of the 1980s, the Roman authorities began to seize the initiative from the regional conferences of bishops: to adapt the liturgy to the genuius of the Roman Curia rather than to the genuis of the local peoples. This was an unforeseen devel-opment, perhaps naively unforeseen. An extended illustration of the consequences of this procedural reversal is in order.

In 1990 the widespread shortage of candidates for ordination into the clerical culture is well-known and needs no elaboration here. The scarcity of ordained clergy has become an impediment to the implementation of the vision of *Sacrosanctum Concilium* no. 106 which designates that each Sunday, "the original feast day, " the Christian people are to gather to take part in the eucharist. The constitution specifies that no other celebrations are to take precedence over this eucharistic celebration of the paschal mys-tery. Yet in 1988 a most curious text was promulgated from Rome, a *Directory for Sunday Celebrations in the Absence of a Priest*.

I call it curious. Its vision is narrowly clerical rather than fully ecclesial. It assumes that the church of Jesus Christ has no recourse but to abandon the conciliar plan for the revitalization of the Sunday eucharist, because there are not enough ordained clerics to spread around in the vast multiplicity of liturgical assemblies. It cannot imagine that there is a solution close at hand in every place where the church has taken root, namely, the identification of alternate criteria for suitable candidates for church office and liturgical leadership from among the baptized.

I also call the document dangerous. Many among us are so vulnerable to the authority of the clerical culture that we too cannot imagine the alternative. We clutch the 1988 text to our bosoms as though it were a boon from a king, delude ourselves that Rome is at long last acknowledging the giftedness of the laity, and let our critical faculties be dulled. Why do we accept the clerical premises of the document? Why can we not distinguish between the existence of a clerical elite and the possibility of alternative forms of ordained ministry in the church?

The question is rhetorical. The answer is that we all cower easily in the face of disapproval from high places. A cardinal archbishop of a major northeastern see has regaled gatherings of Catholics in 1990 with the riddle, now all-too-familiar to church professionals. "What is the difference between a liturgist and a terrorist? " Answer: "You can negotiate with a terrorist!" When the laughing is over, is it too bold to say that the Sunday celebration of the eucharist ought to be non-negotiable in the Roman Catholic Church after *Lumen Gentium* and *Sacrosanctum Concilium*and two millennia of tradition?

But there is more Roman-initiated liturgical reform to come. The Roman Curia has promulgated a revised rite of presbyteral ordination which will be available in vernacular translations shortly. This 1990 revision, it should be noted, is not the result of the numerous requests from various episcopal conferences about the need to reflect deeply on the ordained ministry in the light of pastoral reality. Rather, the "new" ordination rites heighten a clerical understanding of church office. This clerical-ized viewpoint takes male profession of celibacy as the radical qualification without which nothing further is possible, and then simply reasserts the theologically vulnerable symbolic theory that only male Christians can image the Risen Christ in the church. Interestingly, the promulgation of the rites preceded the

October 1990 Synod of Bishops convened to discuss the question of priestly formation. There is evidently no expectation that anything new will come of that body's extended reflection on the global church's experience of ministry in the last decade of this twentieth century since the birth of Jesus Christ.

Here we are face to face with one of the hard issues. The liturgical reform process envisioned by the conciliar constitution has been aborted by the Roman Curia; it never had a chance to come to full term. The agenda for liturgical reform and ecclesial renewal has been usurped by the agenda for the preservation of clerical culture. That agenda is currently controlling virtually all decisions about interpretation of existing liturgical books and about requests for adaptation to the genius of local peoples.

Before I explore further this phenomenon that I have been calling clerical culture, let me be clear about what I am not saying. I am not saying that the church has no need for ordained officeholders. On the contrary. But I am saying that church office too is a suitable subject for inculturation, and that the denial of that fact is an obstacle to liturgical reform, church renewal, and the church's dialogue with all other contemporary cultures. I am also saying that clerical culture has a relative and not an absolute value. Like all other cultural achievements, it is to be judged by evangelical criteria, for its aptness in the service of the church's mission to preach the Gospel of Jesus Christ to all nations and to give praise and thanks in Jesus's name.

Clerical culture is a last vestige of the ancient imperial culture of the city of Rome. It has at its root the system of social arrangements that once served a pagan empire. Pre-Christian Roman culture was a culture based on a presumption of the *a priori* preeminence of male elites who hold power by divine right. Power-brokering among male elites was its controlling dynamic. Clerical culture carried some themes of Roman imperial culture to new stages of development. For instance, Roman imperial culture presumed that public roles were the prerogatives of males; women had no place in the power-brokering of public life. The Roman Church has maintained continuity with this unexamined pagan tradition, even when it sometimes finds itself at the end of the twentieth century "delegating" responsbility for the conduct of its public business to the technically unqualified.

In the emergent Roman ecclesiastical culture, celibate males as an elite corps among all males were credited with having special qualifications for brokering divine power. A variety of philosophical and cultural eddies of the ancient world eventually submerged the ancient evangelical faith in the one baptismal call—with odd results. One such result is the notion, vigorously defended right up to the present, that a public profession of male celibacy is the *sine qua non*, that without which one cannot aspire to public office and to liturgical leadership in the Roman Church.

In continuity with the rhetoric of the culture of imperial Rome, clerical culture asserted and continues to assert that its privileged existence and its exercise of absolute power is *ius divinum*, by divine right. It asserts that it is not itself under any judgment, whether human, ecclesial, or evangelical. And so both liturgical reform and ecclesial renewal are stuck. Powerful officeholders identified with clerical culture give greater authority to that past cultural achievement than to present cultural realities. How do ordinary people argue with elite males who claim for themselves—contrary to much of the available empirical evidence about what is going forward in the life of the church—privileged knowledge of the mind of God?

Many people were reading Amy Tan's first novel *The Joy Luck Club* in the summer of 1990, if bestseller lists are reliable indicators. In that novel four Chinese women and their four Chinese-American daughters have their lives set out for our reflection. One of the daughters, Lena, observes her mother Ying-Ying's way of dealing with life: "She sees . . . bad things that affect our family. And she knows what causes them. But now she laments that she never did anything to stop them." Ying-Ying's quiet regret in her old age carries with it unspoken expectations for her adult daughter.

Lena's marriage is as precariously balanced as the slender black vase sitting on the unsteady marble-topped table which helps furnish the guest room where Ying-Ying stays on her rare weekend visits. The mother not unreasonably sets some of her belongings on the table and watches everything crash. To relieve her mother's embarrassment, Lena says to Ying-Ying: "It doesn't matter . . . I knew it would happen."

"Then why you don't stop it? " asks the mother. "And it's such a simple question, " Lena observes as the episode ends.

Then why don't *we* stop what we see happening to our ecclesial communities twenty-five years into liturgical reform and church renewal? It is such a simple question, for which there is no simple answer that I know. That makes it a hard issue to confront. Twenty-five years ago, collection of conciliar documents in hand, we thought we knew where we were going and we thought we would walk the road into the future hand-in-hand: enlightened bishops, enlightened presbyters, enlightened laity. Within a generation or two we would be worshiping in spirit and in truth and ushering in a new era of justice and peace. Illusions exist to be shattered. Now we seem to be left with biding our time.

Biding Our Time as Dialog with the World

Let me characterize our present situation from a theological viewpoint. Our concern is with what a number of theologians are now calling inculturation. Our real challenge is to allow the culture of the reign of God to enter into conversation with the global human culture and the many national and popular cultures of this world at the end of the twentieth century. How do we do that? And how will our doing that have impact on our public prayer?

How do we enter into the conversation of inculturation? What makes the conversation most peculiar is that we ourselves must take on all the roles. It is not as though the church occupied one zone, the high ground, and the world another. All of us, the baptized and the ordained are authentically secular and authentically graced. We have the Spirit of the Risen Christ Jesus dwelling within us. Yet we also are women and men of our own day, both mirroring and embracing the myopic visions of our secular culture.

Twenty years ago in his book *The City of the Gods*, theologian John Dunne observed that every culture is formed in response to the fact of death. Every culture offers its distinctive answer to the human dilemma: "If I must die, what can I do to satisfy my desire to live? " Coming to terms with our culture is another hard issue for us as Roman Catholics in this post-conciliar era. Cultural achievements are manifestations of human creativity, a form of human stewardship of the earth. They are real and satisfying to a degree. But they are always partial in their visions of what will fulfill our hearts' desires. And as feminist theorists have recently made clear, cultural achievements have consistently showed partiality for the heart's desires to society's male elites. But even if we can yet learn to attend to the aspirations of all of us, the masses of women and men, our cultural achievements will take us only so far in our desire to live well. If we must die, what can we do to satisfy our desire to live?

Christians believe that in Jesus we have received a difficult but freeing answer to our search for more abundant life. The way to life is paschal: let go of your life in order to find it. That one answer is good for all cultures; but the one answer poses different challenges to each culture and to different classes and groups within each. What have your settled for as your heart's desire? Are you open to a change of heart?

To the measure that we have put our trust in Jesus Christ as the Way, we are necessarily wary of overrating even the best promises of our own cultural syntheses. So the spirits within our culture must be tested. We must discern and embrace what is of God in the cultural movements around us, for we proclaim the working of the living God in human history even to our own day. We might wish to decline the honor and the responsibility for serious personal participation in this conversation between Gospel and culture, in this discernment of spirits. We might welcome the invitation: Leave the driving, if not to Greyhound, then to the bishops, to the pope, to theologians, to Mother Theresa. Yet we really have no choice except to participate if we wish to maintain our dual citizenship in this age and the dawning reign of God. As Annie Dillard put in her extended essay *Holy the Firm*, "There is no one but us. There is no one to send . . . There is no one but us. There never has been."

And that truth brings us to reflect on the present situation of our liturgical assemblies. Profound inculturation of the Gospel in this culture will take time, for it is only profound transformation of the local church—the church inserted in place and time—which will result in a more authentically inculturated liturgy. Our aspiration is a renewed liturgy which celebrates the paschal message of salvation as the message is manifest in this culture. At this stage of things, it is our regular liturgical celebration, Sunday by Sunday, season by season, that will be the workshop for the

movement from culturally-alienated liturgy to liturgical acculturation and to liturgical inculturation.

Fifty years after the first gathering of U.S. Catholics in the
pre-conciliar liturgical movement, the movement must recon-
stitute itself. I propose a two point program for those of us committed to continuing the work of liturgical revitalization. Let's
call it "biding our time as dialogue with the world." First, press
the implementation of the conciliar liturgical reform in your Sunday assemblies as well as in your other sacramental liturgies
beyond your present level of achievement. Second, monitor your
local assembly's movement toward what we have begun to call
"good liturgy." That monitoring will involve you in theological
reflection, an activity suited to all thinking Christians.

Point One: Press yourselves beyond your current level of
achievement. This is essential. Much of the time we are settling
for too little. The Roma *editio typica* in translation may fall short
of our aspirations for full liturgical and ecclesial renewal. But the
official liturgical books are capable of taking us much farther than
we have yet gone into a renewed understanding of paschal faith.
All of the Vatican II rites are based on the theologically sound
premise that liturgy is the act of the whole church, the whole
community of the baptized. Our celebrations do not yet consistently affirm that truth. Some anecdotes can illustrate the
point.

A woman with a doctoral degree in theology tells me her
Northern Virginia parish does not use women lectors. I asked her
why she agrees to this arrangement, which has no basis in present discipline and is contraindicated by the Roman liturgical
books and the interpretations of the National Conference of Catholic Bishops. I do not remember her answer, because no answer
is credible. All possible answers assume the liturgy belongs to the
presiding priest and is celebrated according to his tastes.

In the spring of this year we buried my mother. The parish-
priest asked if there was anything special the family wanted at
the liturgy. I specified that I wished communion to be offered in
both kinds. He immediately pulled back. "We don't do that in
this parish." I asked if that was diocesan policy, since the liturgical law of the church provides for it? "No, " came the reply, "it's
the pastor's policy." Then he made a cautious and reluctant

pastoral move. "I'll ask him to make an exception. But if we give permission to you, it won't be long before we have to allow it for everyone." Indeed!

The restoration of the cup to the whole assembly of communicants has solid thelogical foundation. The General Instruction of the Roman Missal authorizes it; subsequent interpretations have made that ritual action available in virtually all eucharistic gatherings. That theology will never be explored by this generation, nor its ethical implications probed, if the ritual action is avoided and so there is no need for sound catechesis and sound ritual protocols for the assembly's drinking from the cup.

The communion rite in the General Instruction of the Roman Missal is better than our typical performance in another way.The trip to the tabernacle still occurs with great frequency, although now it is quite likely to be a lay communion minister who makes the trip. Whoever does it, doling small hosts from the ciborium to communion ministers' plates is more common than the visible ritual breaking of bread which looks like bread. Does anyone among us believe in the sign "one loaf, one body"? But how can they believe when no one invites them to celebrate the sign. Should we decide at the end of the twentieth century to celebrate this ancient doctrine of ecclesial communion in its fullness, it will require catechesis. But a developed catechesis on the eucharist as our sharing in the meal of the kingdom is at the heart of any authentic dialog between church and world. Anecdotal data is unlimited; enough has been cited to make clear my first point: Press yourselves beyond your present level of achievement in the implementation of Roman liturgical books.

Point Two: Look carefully and think deeply about what is being valued as "good liturgy" in your parish. Recently a group of liturgical researchers reported that what was the most commonly identified criterion for measuring "good liturgy" in the United States twenty-five years after Vatican II was celebration that satisfied participant's need for human community. In our late twentieth-century culture characterized by the disintegration of major social institutions, racism, individualism, and self-promotion, community is indeed "good news." The Gospel of Jesus gains a hearing among us by speaking to our deepest hungers. We want to belong, to participate, to have a name and to count in an otherwise impersonal mass society.

But when we ask community-satisfied people to report how the value of community finds expression for them in their Sunday assemblies, the data is telling: sharing coffee and doughnuts after the liturgy; a Christmas eve birthday party for the baby Jesus complete with cake and cocoa; the reading after communion of the names of both adults and children who will be celebrating birthdays, followed by a round of "Happy Birthday." My ritually curious mind wants to know: how is the communion rite being celebrated in such assemblies? How can ordinary food and drink and song satisfy our deepest yearnings?

The reported phenomena are more properly identified as expressions of acculturation than inculturation of the Gospel of salvation. Acculturation is a surface harmonizing of the customs of the people with the values of the Gospel. It predisposes us to hear the word in its fullness. Acculturation is nothing to be spurned. But it is not yet authentically paschal in its impact. We do not hear resounding in an acculturated liturgy a strong answer to that gnawing question: If I must die, how can I satisfy my desire to live?

What more might be expected of a liturgical performance that gives symbolic expression to the mystery of a people alive in Christ? There is no single answer. But the answer is more likely to be found in our performance than in the pages of the books themselves. I believe we must risk more in naming and facing the human questions with which people are struggling than we commonly do when we come together for public prayer. Seated side by side on the benches of every assembly are our cultural crises with human faces: meet nationalism, racism, sexism, individualism embodied in their consequences. Meet the pain of the crisis of affordable housing, teenage pregnancy and teenage suicide, white collar crime and corporate greed, homophobia and unwanted pregnancy, and the exile of political refugees gathered around the table of the living God. How do we celebrate? What do we celebrate?

The Easter Vigil I attended this year was such a high risk liturgy. The inner city parish had no baptisms for the first time in several years. But it had experienced a resurrection to new life in another way, and it recognized the mystery of its visitation. But most importantly, it dared to celebrate publicly Christ's victory over death as they had lived in it.

"What's happening?" my ritually curious mind asked when the pastor yielded the presider's place to his associate, a slight, mild man not yet forty years of age who had not presided at a parish Sunday eucharist for well over a year, even when he was occasionally present. We knew his story, informed of his progress by the pastor. Alcoholism had brought him close to death because of liver disease. He was neither physically nor emotionally able to preside in the assembly. So the assembly prayed for him in his presence and in his absence, at the pastor's regular bidding. Elderly women of the parish ministered to him during the weeks and months of his illness, by gathering with him for bible reading and prayer. People who knew trouble in their own lives accepted his as normal.

Then, at the Vigil 1990 he took his place at the head of the church gathered to proclaim the power of the resurrection. At the homily, he spoke publicly for the first time in months. He began. "We know the power of Christ's resurrection. I stand among you as one raised from death." He went on immediately to identify the *locus* of grace. He assured his hearers, black and white working class residents of a "city under siege, " that by their faith, their prayer, and their lives, they had the power to restore life to others. He was their witness. Then he exhorted them to use their power within their families, their neighborhoods, their city. The mystery of Easter was palpable. We knew it.

By the norms of the Roman books, our parish celebration was irregular, for we had no baptisms. But we performed the rites and prayed the prayers as best we could. Our ritual participation was admittedly uneven: good readers and droners mixed, a high point when the black deacon effectively rapped the great Easter proclamation, and awkward moments when an elderly parishioner routinely took periods of ritual silence to ask her companion in a stage whisper: "Why is this taking so long?" Yet our overall performance authentically inculturated the Easter mystery in northeast Washington in 1990: here is a people powerful in Christ. Their pastors led them through a celebration where that truth became manifest.

This is not a performance to be replicated, but one to be remembered as a touchstone for the truth of paschal faith. Good liturgy will be liturgy that gives public ritual expression to the mystery of a people alive in Christ. Each such graced experience will teach us to take the Roman books and to use them intelligently to celebrate our living faith. As we have already begun to do this, we are discovering that we need to say more than the authors of the Roman books ever dreamed or imagined.

Our faith and our need have already begun to outstrip our texts and our ritual protocols in many ways. Yet the present books, well celebrated, remain our starting point, our insertion into a living tradition of public prayer. Used intelligently, our official liturgical books can help us recognize precisely where the normative tradition well celebrated still falls short of our emergent understanding of the demands of evangelical faith for late twentieth-century Americans: if we must die, what can we do to satisfy our desire to live? Neither episcopal conferences nor Roman congregations can learn this, except from those who gather in the local churches to celebrate the faith that is ours. At these points, in the gaps between text and the experiences of grace, the need for fuller inculturation will assert itself.

* * * * * *

The English Catholic essayist Gilbert Keith Chesterton described external threats to the church in the sixteenth century, in his poem celebrating "The Battle of Lepanto." After the victory, the reigning pope declared deliverance through Mary, Help of Christians. I grew up in a parish named for Mary under this title. So as a schoolgirl, I committed to memory some lines of the Chesterton poem. They were the voice of God speaking:

> I give you naught for your comfort,
> naught for your desire,
> save that the winds grow stronger and the waves rise higher.

Chesterton's somber rhyme is a sad song. But I offer it as a word of encouragement. After all, we were asked to face the hard issues.

3

Twenty-Five Years On—Seen from the Roots: The Migration of Powers

David N. Power, O.M.I.

It is twenty-five years since the close of the Second Vatican Council, twenty-five years of liturgical revival, of the composition of new texts and ordinals, of the implementation in local churches of the new rites and new vision. It is time for taking stock, for grasping what has been accomplished. It is also time for looking ahead, both by way of planning further and by way of appropriating or assessing the perceptions that have emerged in the course of the twenty-five years. The purpose of this article is to address some issues and needs for liturgical development in the next twenty-five years and beyond, particularly as this pertains to the North American continent. It is not to predict what will happen, but to consider what could happen if certain questions are admitted and trends assimilated. What will happen might of course be the very opposite, since the future depends on how these matters are addressed.

While we naturally rejoice at the revitalization of communities of the baptized, we can hardly help noticing that a number of social groups have not been integrated into the flow. One way of looking to the future is to consider the reasons for this. This will be the first part of the article. Then an attempt will be made to see the issue of worship in the context of a prevailing human crisis in the present course of history. In the third part of the article, in the light of what precedes, some suggestions will be made about future directions for liturgical renewal.

MARGINALITY

Rather than rehearse the changes that have taken place within the liturgy, in terms of looking to the future it may be preferable to look at some factors that circle around liturgical renewal, as it were, that seem to show where the new liturgy does not quite fit. This is not because the new rites are poor in themselves, but because there are features of cultural and religious life that seem to be left out. In particular, there are certain groups of people who have not been drawn into the mainstream of liturgical change. In the end, attention to these groups may have far more to do with liturgy's future than the new books, or the new musical repertory, with all that is good, bad, and indifferent in it.

There are six groups that remain foreign or marginal to what has taken place in the implementation of new liturgies.

Religiously-Minded Youth

Among a number of young people, perhaps born since the Vatican Council, there is a marked effort to retrieve forms of piety, devotion, and worship which have been set aside in the process of reform. Their piety takes a shape which looks like religious conservatism. It is an effort to revive what has been officially abandoned, or at least abandoned in practice, though the effort can be fostered by conservatively-minded church leaders who have never willingly absorbed the reform of Vatican II. Examples among young Catholics are the fascination with the Latin Mass, religious vesture, or exposition of the Blessed Sacrament. The reason for this phenomenon is at least partly linked with the desire of these young people to retrieve the tradition of which they think the previous generation has deprived them, or with their sense that the religious has been as much manipulated as the resources of the earth. In a perhaps unconscious way, they assert that God has become lost in the process of manipulative change. They are sensitive to the fact that traditions are not created out of nothing, and that it may be a weakness of liturgical revision that it has been maneuvered by the technological spirit that says that human reason can start at any moment that it wants, *da capo* as it were, even though with sounds that do not resonate with what went before. Within Catholicism at any rate, what is just as interesting is that young people are attracted by forms of devotion which have never properly belonged within the liturgy, such as the rosary, stations of the cross, the wearing of medals and crosses, and certain kinds of Marian devotion. Though the phenomenon needs to be diversely examined and critiqued, it is worthwhile in the present context to point to a devotional need that the revised forms of public worship do not seem to satisfy, or which they at least awkwardly accommodate.

Life-Cycle Practitioners

There is a peculiar alliance between this reversionism of the devout young and the habits of persons of a rather more ephemeral religious allegiance. For many people, on this continent as elsewhere, Jewish or Christian rites are still the periodic markings of human life in its basic four stages of birth, adolescence, marriage, and death. Their relation to synagogue or church may or may not be authentically religious, but it is more social than ecclesial, in the sense of identifying themselves with communities of faith. Rather than being satisfied with purely civil ritual that marks these moments for many Americans, these people want to retain the religious factor, however oblique or vague this may be for them, however profound or superficial. Such people also tend to hold to the few annual observances, such as Christmas and Easter, Hannukah and Passover. In this regard, a pastor of a Catholic parish once remarked to me, rather ironically, that the parish could not afford too much success with its Easter Vigil, since there would be no way of accommodating on Saturday night all the people who show up in church in the course of Easter Sunday. In their own way, these seasonal Catholics would like to revert to an earlier time when this kind of religious adherence was not met with the exigencies of stricter demands.

Has our liturgical development in fact failed to respond to the religious interest of such members of our religious bodies? Even though we know that the dispensation of Christian sacrament is not tied to these points in life, indeed even deliberately evades them, they remain points at which by word and ritual the Gospel enters human existence. They are vital points of human "excentricity," at which either traditions may stiffen or calls to conversion may be heard and life transformed. Is the church, in its testimony and in its worship, truly able to embrace humanity at these vital points, leaving nothing behind of what is truly human? While much just effort has been put into the renewal of seasonal and sacramental celebration, much more attention has to be given to the liturgies that invite the adherents of the life-cycle into the Gospel and the church. Such celebration is also part of the church's mission and integral to its life as a redeeming community.

Devotees of Popular Rituals

In the lives of many people, the popular expressions of faith or religion that grew up over the centuries of split between official liturgy and the nonliturgical, are still more vital than revised rites and practices. Times of fast, the Good Friday way of the cross or devotion to the dead Christ, Ash Wednesday services, pilgrimage, the popular elements surrounding Hannukah or Christmas, have a stronger hold than what is in the new service books of church and synagogue. They seem to speak to a need that is left untouched by liturgy, and they may also carry expressions of faith that could enliven the liturgy at its dead points, offering many a harmonious entrance into the worship of God's people. At times, these popular expression of faith are ones readily adopted by the seasonally religious. They also, however, have a great appeal to some regular church-goers.

The Marginal or Alienated

In the opposite corner are groups of communities that feel alien to parent communities, in their personal lives, in their social commitments, and in their liturgical forms, not because the old has been abandoned but because new exigencies have not been satisfied. Quite often such groups go beyond the prevailing distinctions and divisions between Christian Churches, or between Christians and Jews, or Christian and other religious bodies or traditions. Quite often they are marked by a strong evangelical and contemporary commitment to a way of life that is more

obedient to the foundational orientation of their religious traditions, and at the same time sensitive to contemporary concerns,
such as issues of justice and poverty, the role of women in culture
and society, the truly ecumenical which brings divergent traditions together, and the ecological. Most important among such
acts and rites of worship are those of women's bonding. The
worship of such groups is by basic intention rather free and open,
engaged in a retrieval of faith quite the opposite to reversionist
conservatism. Like any other cross section of humanity, these
groups harbor sanity and madness, but they form part of the
worship of the age and are a prophetic voice.

Lay-Led Communities

For a variety of reasons, some of necessity and some of choice,
more worship is taking place without formally approved or at
least ordained ministers. This seems to be particularly important
in the Roman Catholic Church where what some call lack of
vocations and other rules about ordination have led to an increase in acts of worship led by persons other than the ordained.
In some cases, however, the reality is more a matter of choice on
the part of those who believe that the forms of official approval
are in fact preventive of true renewal, representing as they do
institutional and ideological interests. To these, whatever the
availability of the ordained, less hierarchical liturgies seem to
offer a greater possibility of letting God speak.

Cultural Groups

In religious expression, there is an emergence or new recognition of different cultural repertories, such as Afro-American,
Vietnamese, Hispanic, and Haitian. These ethnic and cultural
groups find that their own forms of religious expression are still
largely marginal to the liturgy, even though some of them now
have their own conventions and their own pastoral plans. The
truly perceptive know that this is not simply a matter of the
language, music, or body-rhythms used. It is more deeply a
question of whether the story is unfolded in such cultures, and
whether the people who unfold the story are going to be appro-

priated into some of our leading Christian Churches. For the present, despite the existence of gospel choirs and Mariachi Masses, the repertory and the people's stories are largely marginal to Roman Catholic liturgy.

I would sum up the exclusion from, or marginality to, liturgical reforms of these groups as symptomatic of what the reform has failed to do. Most impressively, this is a failure to be a liturgy for all people, one that is open to the human in its manifold diversity and its manifold need. Each in a different way, these groups raise questions for us about what has been done in liturgical reform. Each shows something that has been excluded, or that remains marginal to the liturgies of reformed rites. Fundamentally, they ask whether we know what we are doing. They represent needs and interests that ask of their nature to be heeded. In the end, they put a question mark to the church's ability to carry through with a liturgical revision which genuinely embodies the mystery of Christ for all peoples in a congregation of faith.

From a more formal or liturgical point of view, one could say that these phenomena call upon us to rediscover the congregation of faith, whatever it be and whatever its form, as the place where Christ and Spirit bring God present. In the liturgy we must learn that the church shares the story, the sufferings, and the hopes of all, and knows its own destiny bound up with these. We must need learn the ways of attending to people, their faith, and their story. We have to recognize and submit to the power of the divine Spirit that is at work among them. From there we must learn the new ways of turning to the voices of tradition and the voices of the past, if we are to find the holy and the sacred, with great reverence, in forms both traditional and new.

SHARING IN THE HUMAN CRISIS

However, precisely because these phenomena are so varied and represent such a diversity of interest and desire, they point to a deeper crisis, which is the crisis of the human. There is beneath them, and indeed beneath the religious phenomenon as such, something more deep-rooted in society and in culture, to which the religious is related. In effect, religious traditions in the west are simply caught up in a crisis, or find themselves at a critical turning-point, that affects society and culture, but which obviously has its own peculiar manifestations in the religious sphere. There is no doubt that the revision of liturgical rites has been marked by an element of voluntarism, the idea that with proper scientific preparation and with due authority, it is possible to will a new liturgy into being. Ironically, even though the churches tend to bewail the human pride that took over the western world with the enlightenment, the awesome reliance on human thought and human endeavor, it has been rather privy to the same tendency to control its liturgy by proper five-year planning. All the different groups which I have mentioned that remain marginal to this liturgical reform, put fundamentally the same question: Is the vital development of worship not beyond the capacity to plan? Does it not require a more vital or vitally rooted, less mechanistic, growth?

The Opening of Worship to the Human

Obedience to these more opaque laws of growth would in fact be more faithful to an inspiration of the Second Vatican Council that is more deep-rooted than the desire for liturgical change. Marie-Dominique Chenu, up to his death in early 1990, kept insisting that the great insight of Vatican II was to acknowledge that the church is fully and integrally part of human history. Indeed, though the study of liturgy was not his particular field, among the essays in one of the earliest commentaries on the Constitution on the Sacred Liturgy was an article by him on liturgy and the anthropology of faith.[1] On the one side, this means that in imitating the incarnation, the church brings God's presence and the presence of the Word into all human affairs. In the document on the mission of the Second Vatican Council and in liturgical inculturation on other continents, this incarnational principle has been vital.

On the other side, the attention to the human means that the church too is buffeted by the winds of history, that all that affects the lives of stories of human beings in time and in culture, in historical epochs, affects the church. It and its members are as much affected by currents of history, currents of thought, currents of taste, as other institutions and persons. As Yves Congar remarked, the crisis of church institutions and liturgical forms did not begin with Vatican II, nor is the council the cause of all the turns of events of the last twenty-five years.[2] In one way, the council served to make church members more conscious of its own historicity; in another, that very historicity means that in such a rapidly changing world it could not possibly have anticipated these last twenty-five years. In any case, to grasp what is going on in the church we need to grasp the cultural and historical crisis of the time in which we are living, which when it touches forms of worship shows up in part in the exclusion of those noted above.

Most fundamentally, this crisis involves the concept and grasp of the human. In recent theology, particularly that which influenced changes in church performance and in worship, there has been what we call the turn to the human subject, or the concern with the concept of the human which underlies the theology of grace and the theology of God. Our thinking about God, it is recognized, owes much to our thinking about the human. Rather belatedly, the Roman Catholic Church caught up with (or simply took note of?) the respect for freedom, for the individual person, for creativity, that were retrieved by the enlightenment, or modernity, from frozen cultural and religious traditions, rather heavily marked by a desire for order above all else, and by a God significant for orderly behavior. The images and concept of human dignity were of course present in the Scriptures, in patristic writings, and in the great scholastic theology of the high middle ages. They were, however, imprisoned by concepts of order, and it seemed to take a secular tradition of thought to bring the fuller appreciation of the human forth from more rational sources.

The Flawed Human

As the church was, rather belatedly, absorbing something of the culture of the human, others were drawing attention to the failures of this enlightened being. Humanity's attempts to control nature and history, or even to write constitutions that support the quest for life, freedom, and the pursuit of happiness, appear flawed, in some minds even radically so. Some pursue the roots of the flaw into the philosophies that have governed our concept of the human, or into the difficulties that we experience even in reading texts out of the past, or into the paradigms that have governed religious traditions and carried over into the secular. In an appeal for a renewal of faith, one cannot simply say that the loss of a sense of the religious or of the sacred is at the roots of the ills of the time. The religious traditions share and contribute to the flaw.

We find ourselves in a situation in which we know that we need, but do not know how, to find a human order that over-comes the discriminations, religious and cultural, of centuries, that breeds a better affinity with nature, that realizes the discontinuities of history and hence realizes that however much we desire to be the agents of our own history, history happens beyond our control. There are forces greater than the human, and a judgment on the human, that seem to be built into the historical, acknowledged even by many who have no desire for the return of religious faith.

Massive and damaging technological control of human life and natural resources is laid at the door of the concept of the human as free, creative, scientifically competent. The Holocaust of the Jewish people and other acts of genocide or human deprivation are seen to call confidence in human goodness into question. In face of this, in some quarters there is a nostalgic return to a mythic sacred, to an ideal of the human as one in its breathing with nature, to cultural models of interdependency and order, and indeed to a persuasion of an original sin that renders the human prone to excess and vagabondage, able to be led out of its dilemma only by being submissive to authority. Such authority may be prized as constitutional, for those who want to avoid too public a nomination of the divine. It is manifestly divine or ecclesiastical for those who do not shun fundamentalist language.

Modernity

The risk in retrieving a more hallowed vision of the human and what is beyond the human, is that of disposing of the gains of modernity in the effort to counteract the evils of the times. The most fundamental persuasion of modernity was the need to unfreeze scientific, cultural, and religious paradigms that in fact shackled human life and the freedom and dignity of the person. This brought a new persuasion of human dignity and freedom that religious traditions had been unable to foster, at least in practice, and an appreciation for rationality, for broad participation in mapping the future, and for human exploration of the boundaries of creativity, not only scientific but also artistic. Somehow, these gains need to be protected, even in the free admission of fault. Those who are sensitive to the aberrations of religious orders propose that the gain lies in preserving the ability of all to reason and to communicate in a reasonable way, and in finding a human and social order where each person, as well as particular communities, are allowed to have the say in that which more directly impinges on their own lives. This is a rationality tinged by humility, one that knows its limits, and that works within a broadened sensitivity to the galaxy and to vital forces that are there, and not brought into being nor dominated by humankind.

For those who operate out of religious faith, it is a matter of opening ear and heart to the voice of God in all those places where it has been stiffled. It would be totally inadequate to fall back on authoritarianism. It is not the voice of authority which has been quenched. As has been indicated earlier, there are other, less orderly voices which have not been heard. It is they who carry the sounds which bespeak that which human planning ignores, the vital forces that command history in ways beyond exact human control. It requires humility to let even our rituals and acts of worship be shaped by them.

Human Pain

What cannot be avoided is the pain, the pain, in the words of Emily Dickinson, "so utter that it consumes being." Around the time of the Second Vatican Council there was a retrieval of the truth and significance of the resurrection of Christ as mystery. It had been passed off for too long simply as proof of his divinity, the assurance therefore of the completeness of the satisfaction which as the God-Man he offered for sin. Through a renewal in biblical studies and a recovery of early forms of worship, the church was able in its liturgy to realize anew the importance and impact of the Paschal Vigil and the hope of the blessed resurrection. In this way it overcame a certain defeatism, a mere submissiveness before suffering, often associated with the imitation of Christ's death.

If we are truly faithful to the Gospel and the liturgical tradition of the church, in this very hope of the resurrection we shall be able to grasp the force of Christ's pain, of his painful descent into hell, so brilliantly celebrated in the Byzantine liturgy and captured in this century in poetry, such as in this poem of Denise Levertov. Having asked what could be distinctive of the pain of Christ, since others surely have physically suffered more, Levertov traces out in poetic image an insight taken from Julian of Norwich:

> But Julian's lucid spirit leapt
> to the difference:
> perceived why no awe could measure
> that brief day's endless length,
> why among all the tortured
> One only is King of Grief.
> *The oneing*, she saw, *the oneing*
> *with the Godhead* opened him utterly
> to the pain of all minds, all bodies
> —sands of the sea, of the desert—
> from the first beginning
> to last day . . .
> within the mesh of the web, himself
> woven within it, yet seeing it,
> seeing it whole.[3]

Even Thomas Aquinas had a word for this when, in treating of the sacrifice and satisfaction of Christ, he emphasized again and again the immensity of the pain that Christ suffered in his flesh and the immensity of the love which he held in his heart for the human race, knowing that it was impossible to reckon with the immensity of the pain unless one reckoned with the immensity of the love. The pain in the love, and the love in the pain, and thus the fire that consumes it in the solidarity of hope, where "the fire and the rose are one." That is the way of redemption: "To make known in bone and breath (and not die), God's agony."[4]

Under the Sign of the Holocaust

The greatest pain of this century, and the pain that seems to reveal the absurd and the inexplicable and the unendurable of all pain, is the Holocaust of the Jewish people under the Nazi regime. It is a pain too awesome for its recollection, and yet it is a pain that lives even to this day. As the cry goes out so often, we must remember lest we forget. Christian Churches have been at fault in largely ignoring this memory, in not harvesting it. Only recently have there been any efforts by Christians to keep the days of remembrance, Yom Ha Shoah, with the Jewish people. Even this would be only a beginning. For its own sake and for the sake of the power that it has to open us to the dread of all pain and suffering, and to stand before God with the immensity of that pain, this remembrance ought to have a prominent place in Christian liturgies of the twenty-first century. If there is any symbol that tells us of the failure of the human, it is that. If there is any symbol that tells us of the complicity of Christian traditions, it is that. If there is any event whose memory compels us to renew our faith in Jesus Christ, to find ways of expressing it that do not blanche before what God has not chosen, or perhaps has not been able, to do, it is that. And yet it is out of the pain of the humanity that we are part of, out of the hell into which we are willing to descend, that like the Jewish people we find hope anew and above all the ways of proclaiming God's great name. As written on the walls of a cellar in Cologne, Germany, where Jews hid from Nazis:

> I believe, I believe in the sun when it is not shining.
> I believe in love even when feeling it not.
> I believe in God, even when God is silent.[5]

To which we can only add: May God's great name be blessed for ever and ever.

LITURGICAL FUTURES

There is an invitation in this crisis, and in the need to be more fully and genuinely open to the human and its pain, to which we need to respond in worship. In light of it, and taking into account the groups whose lives are scarcely touched by reforms, corporate worship may need to allow for an evolution which would incorporate the following orientations. In fact, they would be in keeping with a recovery of that which is most elemental and vital in liturgical traditions.

Naming the Grief

Communities of faith, whatever the trepidation it causes them, need to be willing to name the dilemma, the sin, the loss of heart, the perplexities that lie at the heart of the human crisis. This can be done within the two most fundamental acts of worship, namely, telling tales and blessing God.

Central to all worship is the Christ story, but to become the human story it needs to merge with other stories. Early Christian centuries allowed for the tales of the martyrs in their liturgies. In these stories Christians found the continuing evidence of Christ's presence, and of the ways in which Christ's story unfolds in the human story. There is room for testimonies in our liturgies. What is different, is that the human story for us is more enigmatic. Rather than take only what is canonized, corporate worship has to be able to absorb the full human story, to hear the witness of what is spoken or cried forth in every quarter, and to listen to Christ's voice within it.

Enough is now known about the blessing tradition to allow it to organically incorporate these stories and the desires that flow from them. It has been repeatedly said that the eucharist of Christian commemoration has roots in the Jewish practice and forms of blessing. Like everything else, this gets stereotyped and the necessary parts and boundaries are prescribed. However, recent studies have delved enough into the Jewish tradition to let us suspect its power to incorporate even the unfinished story, the enigma of sin and suffering, while still praising and blessing God.[6]

Furthermore, the church has to appreciate that all blessing has its paradigm in the eucharist, and that blessing belongs in every key sacrament and liturgy. Taking the same pattern of recall of God's deeds, naming human sorrow and affliction, thanking and praising, confessing sin and faith, invoking the Spirit and the Spirit's gifts, communities have yet to discover the power which blessing can have in a liturgy of penance, where the confession of sin, confession of faith, and confession of praise join, in the overflow of a story where sin too is named, as well as redemption. They also have yet to discover its power in a blessing of the sick which knows how to name from what, beyond the physical illness, the sick of our world suffer, as they have to continue to probe, beyond the questions of canonical form, the forms and content of nuptial blessing within a community of faith.

Voices

If story and blessing are to bring people and their story into Christ, and Christ into their story, it is mete as an integral part of worship to listen to the voices of the oppressed and marginal. All have to invoke the voices of the victims of the Holocaust, as John Paul II did at Mauthausen.[7] Looking, as it were, behind the Holocaust to what preceded and presaged it, we are compelled to heed the voices of those excluded from human history, of the vanquished, of the victims of the success and hubris of others. Liturgy will surely (would that it be so) within the next twenty-five years be at the point to learn from and assimilate the recovery of woman's story, with all the pain and sorrow that this must necessarily entail. Is it also possible to go beyond liking or disliking gospel music, to actually hearing in corporate worship the stories of Afro-American, Indian, Hispanic, and Haitian peoples, as the very condition of being one community with them in faith and in Christ? There are so many to be remembered as we remember Christ, as the very condition of our remembering Christ's cross in truth and fidelity. But the liturgy has that power, simply because its fundamental forms are those of narrative and confession, confession of sin and praise and hope, within the blessing confession of faith.

The Things of Worship

Very much allied with the willingness to hear the full human story, is the readiness to listen to the things that worship has put at the heart of worship—bread, wine, oil, and water. This is where that true reverence that is at the heart of the sacred occurs. The demand is not met by such expediencies as installing a hot tub for baptism at the Paschal Vigil, or finding honeyed recipes for unleavened bread. If the things of earth have voices of their own whereof to speak to to us of human strife and human hope, or of earth's own trouble and groaning, or of horizons of nature beyond our gaze, where they come from and how they are brought to bath or table or bedside, is as important as their presence. We attend to the sonority of water, to the sparkling vivacity of wine, to the textures of bread, and to the sweet fragrances of oil, to their holy and blessed forms. We attend also to the drought of water, to the earth's struggle to produce bread, to the flow from the winepress, and to humankind's bonding with earth in strife and in joy. Heard thus amply, these daily things are the most powerful elements to bring us into God's incarnation.

They likewise allow us to connect church blessings and home blessings, to go from congregation to households of faith, and from households of faith to congregation. Some of the more practically important books of the liturgical renewal are those that contain elements fitted for home use, such as the book for the pastoral care of the sick, and the book of blessings—in the section that contains domestic blessings that serve to complete the daily round or enhance the festive occasion, or complement the more formal liturgies of infant baptism, marriage, and funeral. These blessings should not be carried off as word rituals, but can be expanded to incorporate for their part the things of table, water and oil, as well as the use of hand and body. Reverence and the sacred surround these simple things, and are indeed embodied in them. Christ is ever to be known in the wayside inn of the breaking of the bread, in the jug of wine offered to travelers and to homecomers, in the jar of water at the well of the woman broken off from village life, or in the comforting of anointed limbs where the gentle action of Mary is repeated now upon his members. As the poet Rilke cries out in a phrase seeking a poem:

If for just one day, we only knew
what bread is . . .[8]

Word

It is in the midst of the audacity to hear human voices, and in
the treasuring of life fostered by earthly things, that the word of
God is to be heard. The power of the word actually becomes more
forceful when we allow its doctrinal synthesis and its wonted
readings to break down somewhat. It is to be listened to like a
symphony that breaks the symphonic rules and ushers in a new
era of musical history, like a novel that plays with words in its
disruption of sacred rules of usage. It resonates in lives in new
ways. Deconstructionism does not destroy the power of texts. It
makes them brilliant with new sounds, but digging deep into the
heart of the listener. Looking back, Yves Congar remarks[9] that
one of the most telling or symbolic moments of the postconciliar
epoch was the funeral of Paul VI, of him who had wrestled so
much with the conciliar and anticonciliar forces, and at bottom
with the dilemmas of modernity, of the human creature awakening out of its ambition, realizing in suffering and pain that it is not
the center, not the creator, not the enactor of its own history; that
humanity must find a more humble place within its own history,
more attentive in its struggle to what moves it and what is spoken
to it.

Congar recalls the scene of the plain wooden coffin laid upon
the cobbled pavement. Here, without adornment, is our simple
humanity, in all its feebleness, in its nudity, not only before God
but before the world, the human person reduced to the stark
terms of powerlessness and poverty. That is how humankind is
caught in the winds of change, in the winds blowing across the
square and enhancing the sorrow and the turmoil of all who had
witnessed this life and this death. On top of this wooden box in
which lie the mortal remains of Giovanni Battista Montini, there
lies an open Bible, God's word setting its seal on the testimony of
the servant of God. The leaves of the book are turned by the wind
that blows across the square, those same winds that blow with
unexpected twists across the face of history, opening the book at
places that we ourselves have not picked but to which the Spirit
bids us attend.

Some examples of this affinity with human pain in current readings of the Bible have become known to us. Others await us. Between the leaves of the story of Moses, we have read the story of Miriam. Among the valiant defenders of Hebrew faith, we have found Shiphrad and Puah. Though often neglected in the choices made on the night of the Pasch, the story of Isaac bound, son of an uncomprehending father and sorrowful mother, keeps on reclaiming attention in face of innocent suffering. As we read of the origins of the eucharist, the story of the washing of the feet imposes itself as John's eucharistic testament.

Thus the Infinite plays, and in grace
gives us clues to His mystery.[10]

Devotions

Attending to the devotions that capture the heart and the religious imagination, we find ourselves drawn into new possibilities of marking the festal Christ. So many of these have been born of people's piety, or of the bread with which they fed themselves when ignored by ecclesiastics, or in the midst of their pain and struggle, that they have a deep-rooted seat in the human story and in human suffering, in that of lives often unadmitted to the liturgy. The matter is well put by Mary Collins:

Devotional impulses seem to gain intensity at points where liturgy is hard-pressed to meet the peculiar challenges of the dominant culture of the larger society. Where liturgy is resourceless, the people nevertheless supply in some way . . . Imagination, not desperation, is the more appropriate response for liturgists to bring to such moments.[11]

Some of this devotional occurs in what I have referred to as marginal communities, and Collins gives the good example of the devotion to the motherhood of God which in the past, as in the present, flourished and flourishes outside liturgy. However, I would like to draw attention to the more particular need to respond to that devotional which to a large extent existed for centuries prior to the Vatican Council and which has survived beyond it, finding a home in people's lives which liturgy has not

gained. In looking at such devotion, one would also have to take
account of those situations in which there is a link between devotional intensity and a life deprived of socially fostered human
resources of any kind, be these material or educational.

Without being able here to take up this kind of socio-economic
analysis, it is at least apparent that there are very concrete issues
involved in receptivity to the devotional, reminiscent in way of
the '50s debate as to whether a rosary said in common could be
called liturgy, since it was after all the people's way of remembering the mysteries of Christ. Instead of respect for this, in the late
'60s we had priests breaking rosary beads in the pulpit.

What would you do even today in a parish where the stations
of the cross or the procession of the dead Christ attracts the
greatest crowds during the three days of the triduum? Are these
people not celebrating Easter? Is their devotion really that far
from a liturgical piety that centers on the mystery of Christ's
Pasch? The present form of the paschal triduum began with the
devotions of the Jerusalem populace but, as even a reading of
Kenneth Stevenson's *Jerusalem Revisited*[12] shows, the form has
been revised time and time again throughout history as the devotion to the cross, to the sacraments, and to the Risen Christ took
different shapes among the people of a culture or region. Our
tendency is to fix the ritual of these days in books and make it so
sacred a tradition that we cannot move with the devotions of our
own populace but invite them instead back to an imagined Jerusalem, when what they seek is a Nazarene who has journeyed
from those holy places and belongs to them, who if he is to be
tempted again will be tempted in their midst, if he is to suffer
again will suffer in their midst, if he is to die again will die in their
midst, if he is to conquer death again will conquer it in their
midst.

To take another concrete example, can we let Ash Wednesday
begin Lent even as we insist on the importance of the Sunday
assembly? At times I have toyed with the idea that this service be
transferred to the first Sunday of Lent, as we have transferred
Epiphany and Corpus Christi, to convenience the faithful who
cannot make church on weekdays. Then, of course, I realize that
in effect we have done away with these latter feasts. Perhaps
there is a logic in the choice of the weekday, when people want

it so, just as in earliest times they chose the first day of the week rather than the Sabbath. Ash Wednesday might in fact be the great day for diffusing the call of Lent into the working-place and into homes. In my boyhood days in Dublin, the ceremony of the ashes was one of the few liturgies that literally came home and was a family service. Only the faither of the house went to church, in the early hours of still dark mornings. With him he carried a plain envelope, which he brought with him to the altar-rail to be filled by the priest, as his own head was marked with the sign of the cross. Returning home, it was his turn to mark his wife and children, with the solemn words, "Remember that thou art dust and unto dust thou shalt return." Throughout that day, until nightfall, adult and child gloried in the ashes on their forehead, plain signs for them that they were going to live the next six weeks in communion with the suffering Savior, awaiting the ringing of the church bells on Holy Saturday noon that announced a new spring for the world. In short, oil, holy water, ashes, blessed bread, Ukranian Easter baskets, with the devotion that attends them, bring home the faith and what our liturgies celebrate, and merit being considered an integral part of a Christian people's celebration of Christ's mysteries.

Assemblies without Order

In many places now, voices can be heard that decry Sunday eucharistic services without ordained minister. There is a fear of Protestantization of Sunday liturgy, of the displacement of the eucharist from the community that celebrates to the "thing brought in," of the rendering unnecessary or even absurd of ordained ministry. Yet this is but one further occasion of many sacramental liturgies celebrated without priests, liturgies in which the confession of faith prevails over the lack of hierarch.

The matter cannot be understood by attending primarily to the thing, or the sacramental element. The question is rather whether this action is a eucharistic action, one in which Christ is present in the midst of a community that commemorates his Pasch and blesses God in the gift of the element, wherever it comes from and whatever has been done to it before. The people in the congregation are blessing this bread, blessed though it be as body of Christ in another community of faith, as they remember Christ, invoke the blessing of the Spirit on their assembly and their table, and bless God. The blessing of God, the invocation of the Spirit, the blessing of the bread, and Christ's presence in this sacrament converge. It is the people's pain that they cannot bless their own bread, that they must still take what is given them by another, that they even have to foreshorten the words of remembrance, in short that their own congregation and its celebration have not been given the ultimate sanction of recognition by the ordination of its ministers. Nonetheless, their proclamation of the word, their remembrance of Christ and of those whom they include in Christ, belongs to a reality of church that centers on the formation of eucharistic communities, of communities of word and sacrament and communion in evangelical witness, communities in short of the baptized, of the priestly and kingly people washed in Christ's blood. Their prophetic sound is that, given the reality of the congregation in faith and sacramental act, it ought to be given the seal of order and a fully recognized part in the communion of all the churches, in the one faith, the one hope, the one Spirit, the one body of Christ.

* * * * * *

Perhaps the right moment for this canonical approval has not come until steps are being taken to attend to all the other factors mentioned above. That these communities flourish around the world, without the gift of order, may well be the ultimate sign of the migration of powers that marks the life of the church and can benefit future liturgical history. The realities with which I introduced this study are symptoms of a deep crisis in religious traditions as they share in a deep crisis of human history. They are also, however, symptoms of the recovery, of the need to look in new places for the Spirit of God, indicators of the ways in which in the midst of pain, and the hope born in pain, we may continue to praise God, and in praising find redemption. Drawing out from some reflections on this crisis, I have dared give some indicators of a liturgical future that we can glimpse in the light of the present. There is an inevitable breaking and tearing as the new emerges. In faith, religious people have to dare to acknowledge God where God speaks, even if in whispers, they have to dare to bow in reverence before the new places and persons, to listen to the new voices, to grasp the new theophanies. The challenge is one which comes in face of a migration of powers.

> Often a mask empties itself before believers
> and suddenly the idol apologizes
> for its deceitful throne, for its fantastic pomp,
> for its shrill and common gold.

> Some of our gods become exhausted and withered,
> arid and stiff;
> into others, while murmuring, tumbles the fresh spring
> of a refreshed divinity.[13]

Notes

1. Marie-Dominique Chenu, "Anthropologie de la liturgie," in *La Liturgie après Vatican II,* edited by Jean-Pierre Jossua and Yves Congar (Paris: Editions du Cerf, 1967) 159–177.

2. Yves Congar, "Moving towards a Pilgrim Church," in *Vatican II Revisited by Those Who Were There,* edited by Alberic Stacpoole (Minneapolis: Winston Press, 1986) 129–152.

3. Denis Levertov, "On a Theme of Julian's Capter II," in *Breathing the Water* (New York: New Directions Publishing Corporation, 1987) 68f.

4. Levertov, "The Showings: Julian of Norwich, 1342–1416," ibid. 76.

5. Taken from *Liturgies on the Holocaust,* edited by Maria Sachs Littell (Lewiston, NY: The Edwin Mellen Press, 1986) 40.

6. Among the important works, see Joseph Heinemann, *Prayer in the Talmud: Forms and Patterns* (Berlin & New York: de Gruyter, 1977); Cesare Giraudo, *La Struttura Letteraria della Preghiera Eucaristica* (Rome: Biblical Institute Press, 1981).

7. John Paul II, "The Visit to Mauthausen," *Origins* 18 (1988) 124.

8. Rainer Maria Rilke, *The Complete French Poems,* translated by A. Poulin, Jr. (St. Paul: Graywolfe Press, 1986) 373.

9. Congar, "Moving towards a Pilgrim Church" 148.

10. Levertov, "Variation on a Theme by Rilke," in *Breathing the Water* 71.

11. Mary Collins, *Called to Prayer: Liturgical Spirituality Today* (Collegeville: The Liturgical Press, 1986) 54f.

12. Kenneth Stevenson, *Jerusalem Revisited* (Washington, D.C.: The Pastoral Press, 1988).

13. Rilke, "The Migration of Powers," *The Complete French Poems* 335.

4

Music at the Crossroads:
Liturgy and Culture

Eugenio Costa, S.J.

In a sense, I want to address the kind of roadways you and I are working on the end of the second millennium of Christian history. Like good road builders, we have to know our materials, otherwise we will build as foolishly as people who build on sand instead of a solid foundation (see Mt 7:26). And if we don't know the purpose of our construction, we may create too elaborate a road, with too many exit ramps or traffic lanes, laid down on shaky foundations, and find ourselves broken and bankrupt by our over-elaborate plans (see Lk 14:28–30). The material we will examine is the music we implement in worship; the structural plan for rendering that music is provided by the structure of the rituals we use to praise, thank, and petition God. And the special eyeglasses we will put on to examine all of this is the set of *Universa Laus Guidelines*, from which I will quote extensively.

I refer at length to this document because it provides the best set of "eyeglasses" I have found for focusing on music in worship and for understanding where we should be headed as people concerned with music's role in liturgy. These Guidelines have been around for ten years now; those who worked to develop them and those who have followed them during this time have proven their value. For some points I want to make, I can find no better way to express what I want to say than to quote from these Guidelines.

In looking at the structural role of music in worship, I want to examine four points: (1) where the music comes from; (2) what the "blueprints" of our worship have to tell us about the way we use that music; (3) the problems raised by the blueprints about our use of music; and (4) where we go from here.

Where Does Our Music Come From?

Here is the truth of the matter: Everything is secular, but everything can be used to celebrate Jesus Christ.

If I go into a church on Sunday morning and find a gathering of Christians preparing to celebrate the eucharist, what do I find alongside me and around me?

First and foremost, I find people: men and women, children, teenagers, adults, and senior citizens. The building itself catches my attention. It is built in a specific architectural style. It has paintings, statues, benches, and pews. Electricity provides lighting, sound amplification, air conditioning and heating. Flowers, colorful decorations, background music, and Sunday dress add interest and excitement to the atmosphere.

Then someone begins to speak in my native language. But on this particular Sunday a group of Christians visiting from another country is also present, so the speaker makes them too feel welcome by greeting them in their native tongue. Then the singing begins. The choir sings a verse and the whole assembly sings the refrain, accompanied by musical instruments of some sort. Passages from the Bible are read, prayers are said, more hymns and petitions are voiced—all of this in the vernacular.

Now all these things—people, building, art, speech, song, music—are simply secular before they become Christian. The assembled people, their culture, and hence the cultural raw materials making up the liturgical situation and action are secular before they become anything else. Here "secular" does not necessarily mean "profane," "mundane," or "nonreligious." It simply means "of the world," "of this age," "of this culture." The world, its inhabitants, and their cultures—which are the offspring of human beings and their societies—derive both from the hand of God and from the elaboration wrought by human beings. They bear the imprint of creation's goodness as well as of human work, but the work of human hands may produce both good and evil. Human beings and their culture are the raw materials, often ambiguous and ambivalent, which the liturgy will shape, giving them its own peculiar form.

For me, then, "secular" has profoundly human connotations. In the Christian view of humanity, "secular" embodies the values of divine creation as they have been transformed, for good or ill, by human intervention. Human beings are still quite capable of creating and doing good, but they are also wounded and vulnerable beings, hence equally capable of the most wretched and perverse actions. And much like the human beings who have given birth to them, cultures bear this very same ambiguity within themselves.

The *Universa Laus Guidelines* (ULG) point out that in order to become part of the liturgical action, human beings are called to live the evangelical experience, "which simultaneously includes collective memory—traditions, conversion, and the expectation of the Kingdom" (ULG #2.3). In other words, if the celebration is to be meaningful, it must be carried out in faith. The assembly normally is made up of people who have accepted the gospel message and converted to the God of Jesus Christ. These people are the first and only human subjects of the ritual action. In and with them Jesus Christ exercises his priesthood (see *Sacrosanctum Concilium* [SC] #7).

Like human beings, human cultures must also undergo some sort of process of Christian initiation that will allow evangelical values to be inculturated in them. Singing and music are part of human culture. When they enter the liturgy, they become integrated into an activity that tends "to manifest the newness of Christian salvation. For the faithful, the use of music in the liturgy cannot be considered solely as a product of the surrounding culture. Its use is continually questioned and challenged by the evangelical experience" (ULG #2.3).

Herein lie the ideal and practical roots of the conversion required of singing and music as products of human culture, when they become part of the liturgical action. But that should not lead us to aim for artificially different music or strange, individualistic, and esoteric processes of composition and performance. Like the faithful who rely on them, singing and music are in this world even if not of this world (see Jn 17:14, 16, 18).

When the faithful manage to "evangelize" their culture, that culture (including its singing and instrumental music) is ready to enter the liturgy. To become liturgical, music must always undergo "choices and changes." The Guidelines continue: "The musical practices of a given culture are not all equally available or immediately usable in the liturgy." Moreover, "the liturgical celebration may welcome or require practices that the current musical culture is not familiar with, or has let atrophy" (ULG #2.6, 2.7) Take, for example, the recitative, which is absent from much of nonpopular musical culture in the west, but which is indispensable for psalmody in the liturgy.

In other words, viewed from the standpoint of the liturgy, a given musical culture can reveal a lack of certain musical forms. In short, anything can serve the liturgical celebration, but "Christian assemblies use various kinds of music in a manner that is unique to them" (ULG #2.3). Two Convictions affirmed by Universa Laus read: "Christians do not have a musical form that is distinct from those of other people; but they use each form of music in a way that is peculiar to Christians" (ULG, Convictions,VIII). "No music is in and of itself profane or sacred, liturgical or Christian; but there is ritual music in Christian worship" (ULG, ibid., IX). And again: "Even though, over the course of their history, various churches acquire repertoires that they consider uniquely theirs, there is no specific music for the Christian liturgy" (ULG #2.2).

What Requirements Must be Met for Music to Become Christian Ritual Music?

Clearly, music *for* the liturgy must be music in the liturgy. Not a music that is generically "sacred" or "religious," but a music that fits the ritual action *like a glove*. If we want to spell out the characteristics of ritual music, we must start from the blueprint— from the rite, and not from the music.

Until the reform effected by Vatican II, the problems of "sacred music" were merely problems of style, of sound, of rejecting a generically profane quality and looking for a generically religious quality in music.

The liturgy itself, however, had to be reformed first. Only once that was done could singing and instrumental music be asked to make some effort to fit snugly into the liturgical action. Today, ritual music is no longer the soundtrack of the sacred spectacle. Rather, it is one of the ways in which the assembly celebrates the mystery of Christ. Like word, gesture, and action, singing is one of the basic, elementary forms of ritual expression. Instrumental music accompanies the singing or creates an atmosphere, but it remains closely tied to the liturgical action.

Such liturgical action has its own requirements. We cannot celebrate Christian liturgical worship in a confused way, without objectives or rules—we need, as I said, a "blueprint." The liturgical act is rich and many-faceted. It asks those celebrating it to achieve certain goals and to use appropriate means in the process. To celebrate means to express one's deepest feelings, to create unity in the assembly, to be festive. It also means to teach and to learn, to heal, and to cure. And, in addition, it means to proclaim, to praise, to dialogue, to supplicate . . . to move about, to walk, to dance, and so forth.

All these actions can be called "functions." The Guidelines say: "Liturgical music has a certain number of . . . functions . . . but inasmuch as music is a part of Christian celebration; as such it plays a specific role and fills a certain number of functions that are proper to music" (ULG #7.1).

The first and primary task of singing and instrumental music in the rite is to fulfill these various functions in musical terms. In the liturgical rite, then, song and music are "functional" in two senses: (1) they do not enter the liturgy with a separate personality of their own, with the impact of a foreign body; (2) they arise out of each concrete liturgical action, when it is timely and necessary, and they faithfully fulfill it in musical form.

Among the various ritual functions of singing and music we can distinguish these four: anthropological functions, specifically liturgical functions, aesthetic functions, and finally, ecclesial functions.

First, anthropological functions "that are the same as the general functions of music in society . . . some of them are quite general: music is used for emotional expression, group solidarity, as a ceremonial symbol, and so forth. Others are more defined: therapeutic, instructional, *homo ludens* (man at play), etc." (see ULG #7.1).

Second, specifically ritual functions, which are of two types:

The first are defined, in the sense that particular effects, more or less controllable, are intended . . . Defined functions are of interest to people connected with the liturgy (composers, planners, implementers). In effect, the successful execution of a celebration depends on the defined functions. In the same way that some music is appropriate or inappropriate for dance or relaxation or singing in a choir or for private enjoyment, the field of liturgical music contains that which is appropriate or not for the various expressive acts (proclaiming, meditating, psalm singing, praise, acclamation, dialogue, litanies). To each function correspond different forms, which influence the effect of music to varying degrees [ULG #7.3].

These defined liturgical functions are *strictly ritual* functions.

The other set of ritual functions are indeterminate and their effects are largely unpredictable . . . the role of music extends well beyond its observable functions. As a sign and a symbol, it is a link to something other than itself. It opens the door to the indefinite realm of meaning and free feelings it suggests. Taken in terms of faith, music becomes both the sacramentum and the mysterion of the realities being celebrated by the faithful [ULG #7.4].

These liturgical functions are more in the nature of spiritual functions. In addition to anthropological and liturgical functions, there are also aesthetic ways for music to function. The *Universa Laus Guidelines* say this:

Throughout the Church's history, there has been a twofold concern, on the part of authorities and practitioners alike, with ritual forms, and especially musical forms. The first part of the concern is expressed in terms such as dignity, beauty, appropriateness, good taste, quality, pure art. The second part, tied to the first, is more explicitly religious. It has to do with the holiness of the act, which has to be "prayerful" and "sacred." The search for "beautiful" and "holy" liturgical forms is not so much a matter of aesthetic or ethical norms, which are always relative, as it is a matter of values and "non-values" of a group in its celebrations—what the group recognizes as compatible or incompatible with the liturgy [ULG #9.1–9.2].

Fourth and finally, there are ecclesial functions that music performs. It is useful to recall here that singing and instrumental music, besides their direct use in the liturgy, can also be used at various other moments in the believer's life in the Christian community. For example: when he or she makes first contact with the community and is welcomed into it; when the first proclamation of the gospel message is made, or during any form and level of catechesis; when attempts are being made to express the sense of fraternal life in any of many possible ways; and in particular, when the Christian community gathers together to live its own vocation more intensely and to prepare better for its own mission in the world.

For all these moments there can be appropriate music. There will probably be different kinds of music for different moments. It may well be a mistake to mix up these moments and their corresponding forms of music, but the fact is the songs and instrumental music serving different ecclesial functions are often intermingled in the celebration of the liturgy. This intermingling has deleterious effects and does not help to solve problems. Thus the vocation of liturgical composers is to know the individual rites in depth and to create vocal and instrumental music that flows out of the inner reality of a given rite and its functions.

The vocation of ministers and directors of liturgical chant is to choose appropriate chants and to perform them with the assembly in such a way that they perfectly meet the requirements of the specific ritual act and the dynamics of the whole liturgical action.

The vocation of the participants in the assembly is to enter wholeheartedly into the musical action and to be fully involved in it, when the celebration calls for it. When, and if, all these conditions are met, singing and instrumental music will truly and genuinely be ritual on the printed page and as actually performed. And the ritual character of singing and instrumental music will be concrete, not abstract; they will both be music "appropriate for" the rites in which they are used.

These are the four functions of ritual music that I wanted to highlight—anthropological, liturgical, aesthetic, and ecclesial. Viewing the ritual character of music through these four functions may seem to be too narrow or stifling, but that is not really the case. The wide variety of functions to which composers and those responsible for directing the celebration must respond in their work is a stimulus to their imagination.The whole range of music is needed for the whole range of liturgy. Ritual situations and actions call for the maximum of creativity. Wonderful indeed

is the concrete experience of assemblies gifted with truly liturgical musicians. In such assemblies the rite is vivid and alive;
word, song, instruments, and dance flow beautifully and indeed
very naturally.

Problems Raised by the Blueprints about Our Use of Music.

This is where my title for this presentation comes in, for the
main problem is that music places us at the crossroads between
culture (the raw materials) and ritual (the blueprint). Here is a
problem we cannot sidestep. Let us accept that the ritual functions are the blueprint, the guilding thread; and let us also accept
that singing and instrumental music become ritual through their
complete cohesion with the action of the liturgy. Fine! But what
about the raw materials that song, gesture, word, and music are
made up of? Those raw material come from the most diverse
cultures. They not only have formal characteristics, but also elements of color, accent, character, and connection with experienced situations that profoundly condition them. To put it in
terms of the analogy I used near the start of my presentation,
when we fit the glove of musical material to the hand of the
liturgy, that glove is not neutral. It has its own consistency and
color. It is smooth or rough. It is cut according to a certain pattern.
It may have a nice or a bad smell. Or to put it another way, the
raw material is not "prime matter." It is a product of its formation
and its history. Like the world evoked somewhat negatively in
Gerard Manley Hopkins's poem "God's Grandeur": "All is
seared with trade; bleared, smeared with toil; / And wears man's
smudge and shares man's smell . . ." In liturgical music and ritual
singing, in other words, we find inevitably and already present
a whole series of elements: musical forms, the character of the
melody, the color of the arrangement and setting, the kind of
rhythm, the vocal style.

It is pointless to dream of some kind of idealized music "from
the other world" for the liturgical celebration. When that dream
did get hold of some music experts in the church—and it did so
especially in the latter part of the nineteenth century and the first
part of the twentieth century—it produced what Gino Stefani
describes so well in an article in *Nuova Rivista Musicale Italiana*

(1976, p. 39). He called the works of this period "the immense pile of false Kitsch that the most orthodox sacred music has largely been, among both Catholics and Protestants, during the last two centuries."

Ruling out this solution—discovering some idealized music—we are left with the only other possibility: relating the style in which composers write, the choices of repertoire directors make, and the actual performance of the music to the requirements of the rite, indeed to the ritual functions I discussed above. Here music truly finds itself at the crossroads between liturgy and culture. Any crossroad may mean danger and generate tension and must be approached with great care; but it can also become a place for encounter and sharing.

Assuming that what I said above about rite and its functions is correct, I would like to propose some guidelines or reference-points that might be helpful in working our way through this crossroad. I would like first to look at two erroneous points of reference and then suggest two that are correct.

The first mistaken point of reference that we find when we come to the crossroads is followed by those who look for some way of adapting singing and music sucessfully to ritual by relying solely on a specific repertoire, even a "sacred" one for worship or even adoration. It cannot be done. Just think of the many repertoires that history has bequeathed us: medieval chants such as Gregorian Chant, Ambrosian Chant, and so on; the polyphony of the fifteenth and sixteenth centuries; baroque; the compositions of the classical and romantic periods as well as the twentieth century—on both sides of the Atlantic; and the repertoires of popular music from all ages and cultures. It is an immense sea of music, often quite marvelous. The mistake would be to give absolute, unquestioned priority to one specific author, or corpus of music, or repertoire; to stick to that one choice at any price in our present-day liturgy. That decision would rule out any selection or adaptation, any possibility of making intelligent choices with respect to the individual liturgical rite. The celebration turns into a concert, dealing a death blow to ritual functions as such.

The second erroneous point of reference treats music as a background or spectacle, and it can point us in either of two directions. In one direction we find the decision to go "spiritual," that is, to individualize the liturgy. It is impossible to resolve the tension between the *secular* features of singing and the requirements of the liturgy if we cherish a solely interior conception of the celebration. In such a view music would serve merely as a background for private prayer, and the community rite would be irrelevant. If you lose a precise ritual link, then the music would merely have to be nice, sweet, remote, and somehow "religious" or "sacred." Other aspects and values would have to be excluded, so that a whole part of the people's culture would be cut away.

Following the same reference point, but at the other end of the spectrum, we find those who cherish a view of the liturgy as an exhibitionist spectacle. Singing and instrumental music are meant to be a part of the "show," exhibiting all the emotional power and dynamism they possibly can. The important thing is to induce feelings of excitement and feverishness, even though the focus is religious in this case. Crowd effects and celebrations involving huge masses of people are favored. To achieve these ends, the musicians will use every trick in the book and unscrupulously exploit every resource provided by their musical culture. In this case the spiritual functions of the rite are the ones that are most neglected. There is no room for personal freedom, no opening to the interior life. Everything is already visible and present: *ecclesia triumphans!* Moreover, the cultural touchstones go through no filter as they enter the ritual action, so they end up having a centrifugal impact. It is not the "world" entering the church but the church losing herself, and the celebration doesn't take off.

In contrast to those erroneous guides through the crossroads, I would like to point to two correct reference points: the local assembly and the universal church.

The individual local assembly is a correct point of reference. By that I mean the assembly that gathers in a certain place, on a certain day, at a certain time. This gathering always entails two requirements. First, it must speak its own language, which includes not only the words but also the gestures and movements, the songs and the way they are sung, the musical instruments and the way they are played. In other words, the local assembly should not be transported to an alien world or uprooted from its own tradition; it should not renounce its own cultural heritage. Second, the local assembly must live the celebration in a deep and authentic way, allowing the word of God to speak to it, remaining open to interior change and humbly renewing its covenant with the God of Jesus Christ.

Thus each individual assembly becomes itself the right yardstick for measuring the liturgical quality of all the ritual signs, singing and music included. There is no way to do this except by experimentation, careful and prolonged on-the-spot experimentation. Let me quote from the *Universa Laus Guidelines* again:

> Short of an exhaustive familiarity with the range of believers' reactions—which are usually implicit and inchoate—the musician who is called to serve an assembly still cannot totally ignore its members and their reality. It is useful to the musician, for example, to know which forms they consider to be archaic or modern or out of style; which are considered popular, or elitist, or common; which are good or bad according to experts and/or users; which are sentimental, or austere, or prayerful, or distracting. She/he must know which individuals and groups are concerned about these reactions. Finally, the musician must know whether the criteria are applied more strenuously to the works themselves or to their execution.
>
> In the effort to understand the effects of the musical forms they use, planners of celebrations are not trying to please their public or satisfy their tastes. They define the parameters within which the symbols and the rites of the Christian faith can unfold. They observe the degree to which their meaning is available. Then, together with their fellow believers, they seek the forms that are most likely to foster celebration both in spirit and in truth, without claiming that any individual's values are the only ones or that any individual's taste is the only good taste [ULG#9.3–9.4].

A second correct reference point is the universal church. It is essentially one *and* catholic, differentiated *and* united, plural and one body. It is of basic importance that the individual local assembly should not close in on itself, that it live out its membership in the one great church. It is highly desirable that the local assembly's liturgical celebration, on certain occasions at least, offer concrete signs that somehow render present, ritually as well, all the assemblies of the world and the whole mystery of the one, holy, catholic church. As the 36th Universa Laus Conviction puts it: "Communion among Christians of different congregations, languages, cultures and confessions can be expressed with some common signs, among which music has a privileged role" (UL XXXVI).

Reference to the universal church should take geography and history into account. Geographically, there are five continents, and more than 350 languages in which the Catholic liturgy is celebrated today. Historically, there have been two thousand years and scores of rites or "ritual families"; a huge number of texts and songs.

Here practical examples may be offered: songs in a foreign language or in several languages, chants in Latin or Greek; the use of musical instruments from other countries and cultures; and so forth. This is an important signpost for the church. We should welcome it concretely, in the field of liturgy and music as well, and encourage our assemblies in the direction of "polycultural universality."

Where Do We Go from Here?

I find it hard to go further in spelling out what happens at the crossroads or where our road building will take us. I can only say what should happen, and under what conditions. I know that the crossroads of culture and ritual are getting more complex, for many questions are being posed to us Christians in many nations by our increasingly direct and close ties with other great religions of the world.

May I conclude by urging you to carry on the process of discernment and experimentation. Let us not be afraid of the human cultures in which we were born and raised. But let us also remain alert and demanding when we gather to celebrate the mystery of Christ. As the *Universa Laus Guidelines* remind us: "The ultimate goal of all liturgical expression, and of all ritual, is to manifest and realize the new person in the resurrected Jesus Christ. This accounts for the exigencies of Christian ritual music" (ULG #10.1). "All music created by the people, as long as it is not self-serving or self-reflective, but leads people to the evangelical promise, can serve Christian worship" (ULG #10.2). If the Spirit of God is with us, the very tensions and conflicts that make it difficult to implement right choices in practice can bear much fruit for our celebrations.

5

Theater, Concert, or Liturgy: What Difference Does It Make?

Edward Foley, Capuchin

There is no little irony in what I am about to do, especially considering my belief that American Roman Catholics are increasingly influenced by an entertainment model of worship and my further impression that many pastoral musicians are more and more prone to model their performance styles after those found on MTV or its tamer equivalents. Yet I am also wholeheartedly convinced that liturgy and show business—divine praise and entertainment—are not interchangeable, co-extensive or even compatible genres of human activity. Despite this conviction, however, here I stand: on stage, with special lighting, a sophisticated sound system and the appropriate costume. Furthermore, the expectation of my performance—as I perceive it—is to be informative, inspiring and entertaining. Yet the purpose of this performance, indeed, of these four days of performance, is to enable us to become better ministers and to serve more faithfully the liturgy with our musical art.

The difficult question, however, is whether or not this forum can achieve that goal. Marshall McLuhan's famous maxim, "The medium is the message," suggests that no matter what our words, no matter how impassioned the presentation, this four day event implicitly communicates that worship and entertainment are at least compatible if not coextensive realities. It is a bit like arranging a meeting of Overeaters Anonymous at a Dunkin' Donuts shop, where the air is thick with the sweet smells of bismarcks and chocolate covered eclairs and the environment undermines the purpose of the gathering.

If members of Overeaters Anonymous are going to support each other in disciplining their appetites, they will need the support of an environment which will not overstimulate those appetites. Similarly, if we are to discuss the problem of entertainment models of worship effectively, and if I am to have any success in recommending that we abandon such models for worship, then we are going to need the support of an environment which does not, at least implicitly, uphold the values of entertainment. Quite frankly, however, I am not sure that any American convention these days—political, religious or otherwise—can exist outside of the entertainment model. Thus an unusual dilemma: loving the topic, yet feeling trapped by the medium.

So what are our choices? One possibility is to stop here, though that option hardly seems just or responsible. By accepting the gracious invitation to come to Phoenix, I assumed the responsibility to speak to you, so speak I must.

A second possibility is to try to convince you that only my words and not their performative setting are important. That, however, seems a futile approach for as every 5-year-old knows, "Actions speak louder than words." Liturgists have more sophisticated jargon for this basic insight, but the bottom line is the same: intention alone is insufficient; embodiment is essential. It is not simply what we say but how we say and do and pray that makes a difference.

Maybe the only option at my disposal in the face of this dilemma is a clear and heart-felt reminder that what we do this evening is not worship but convention. Christian worship is about relationships, engaging the community of the baptized in praise and petition to the Holy One through Jesus Christ. Conventions, workshops or other kinds of continuing education, however, are for the development of understanding about liturgy so to enable that relationship in Christ. Though such gatherings may serve liturgy, they cannot replace liturgy and dare not try. Therefore, what we do here this evening is not liturgy but formation for liturgy.

One further disclaimer about our time together in Phoenix: when we do worship together these days, we will not be engaging in parochial worship but in convention worship. That means that we will not be participating in the model of prayer held up by the church for the church but in something unique and, in some sense, elite. The paradigm of worship held up by the church to the church is local, Sunday, parochial worship. It is worship of the people, by the people, and for the people. Or from the viewpoint of the specially trained musician or liturgist it is worship of amateurs by amateurs, always remembering that the title "amateur" does not refer to the level of one's skill but to the level of one's devotion, for an amateur is one who pursues an activity motivated only by love and not out of hope for material gain.

Though diocesan, regional or national conventions might be wonderful oases for those of us who struggle with volunteer choirs and limited local resources, they are neither our goal nor our sustenance. Important as they are for us, we cannot remain on the crest of these liturgical-musical transfigurations. Rather, with the Lord we have to go back down the mountain, back into the city and our local parishes, where the real work of worship and mission is to be found. Without such a perspective we run the risk of trying to sustain the convention liturgy beyond the convention. And when that fails, as it inevitably will, we may be left with the irrepressible urge to find another alien form of worship to impose on our unsuspecting local communities.

BORROWED SYMBOLS

This cautious beginning is an attempt to recognize from the start that the medium does affect the message; to recognize from the start that worship and music conventions in a twentieth-century American mode can create a false model of worship and music that participants may unfortunately attempt to duplicate long after the convention has ceased; and to recognize from the start that it does make a difference if we borrow performance styles from the theater or concert stage and inject them into our worship. And I fiercely believe these things because of two simple and unavoidable principles.

The first principle is that the symbols we employ in our rituals—the music, language, environment, objects, ministries, colors—are never neutral. Symbols do not exist in a vacuum; rather, they exist in a cultural context and they cannot help but transmit cultural values. Thus symbols not only communicate our thought, they shape our thought. Symbols not only help to express our ideas, they also unavoidably transform those ideas, and no power of the will can change that fact. Think of extreme examples: tupperware-style eucharistic vessels with lids that allow you to seal in the bread or wine with vacuum freshness through their patented burp; the Johnny Carson style of presiding, in which the entrance rites of the Mass are replaced by an opening dialogue supported by a deacon who laughs like Ed McMahon; responsorial jingles à la Barry Manilow in which refrains like "I will praise you, faithful God" are sung to the tune of "you deserve a break today." A decision to employ plastic kitchenware for eucharistic vessels, styles of presiding reminiscent of late night television, or jingles for Jesus, are not without consequences. They have implications for the way we understand ourselves and our rituals. Whether we like it or not, symbols not only express our thoughts, they also shape our thoughts.

A second principle follows: symbols not only shape our thought, they also shape our faith. The cultural messages imbedded in every symbol, the commercialism that pervades so many of our twentieth century symbols, have an effect on the rituals that embrace them. Every time we borrow symbols from the surrounding culture for our worship, we not only borrow materials for communicating divine truths, we also invariably shape the divine truths themselves according to that culture.

Innumerable examples from the history of worship make this point. One will have to suffice: an architectural, not a musical example. Initially there was no such thing as Christian architecture. There were only Christians who gathered in spaces to worship. All of those spaces were private and borrowed. Eventually, as Christianity became legal and then fashionable, the growing crowds required larger spaces. One of the most popular styles of public architecture borrowed by Christians was the basilica, specifically the kind used as an imperial audience hall. These large rectangular rooms with a raised platform at one end served the worship needs of Christianity during the great expansion of the fourth and fifth centuries. They also, however, significantly shaped the worship and the belief communicated by the worship. Since basilicas are large enclosed paths, their very shape spawned processions. Thus processions assumed new prominence in Christian worship in the fourth century. The procession of the clergy at the beginning of the worship, for example, was elaborated in ways that would not have been possible in a house-church where people gathered in a single room. Worship was shaped by the building and the ritual conformed to the space. But these spaces not only modified the pattern of the ritual, they ultimately modified the pattern of belief. Processions of clergy, especially the bishop at the beginning of the worship, not only emphasized the bishop's centrality in the liturgy, but also set him apart from the people who did not process in the same way that he did. The raised platform at one end of the basilica became the exclusive place for the bishop, helping to transform him from pastor to ruler. Ultimately this raised platform in the apse became the location for the altar where the bishop performed the holy action while the people were held at a distance. The message of these developments was quite clear: official worship does not belong to the people. They should practice their devotions outside the confines of sanctuary while the monks and clergy accomplish the real worship inside the sacred precincts.

The effects of borrowing that imperial symbol called the basilica are still with us. It is only with enormous effort that in some places communities are becoming convinced that the worship belongs to them. The symbols we employ in our worship—the artifacts, buildings, vessels, and gestures—these are not neutral and they are not without impact upon the shape and meaning of our worship and our faith. And neither is the music.

The Power of Music

You have heard the quotations innumerable times before: the musical tradition of the church is a treasure greater than that of any other art (Constitution on the Sacred Liturgy, no. 112) and music forms an integral or necessary part of the liturgy. Behind such statements is the centuries old belief that music is a powerful ritual force; it has the ability to engage the spirit, move the heart, weaken or strengthen the will, and reveal the divine. As I will try to argue in a forthcoming volume, music is the richest metaphor we have for revealing God in the Judaeo-Christian tradition. It is a potent, mysterious and mesmerizing art.

And there is also its danger, for music's power is not confined to the service of worship, to the revelation of God or to moving the heart to good. Music can conversely inhibit the liturgy, block the revelation of God and move the heart to evil. Since the ancient Greeks the belief has persisted that music has power to sway the mind for good or for evil. It is a belief perpetuated through the ages by philosophers, educators, and ecclesiastics. Belief in the sometimes calamitous effects of music continues even in our own day and many still believe that loud and raucous music is the source of mental disorders and the tool of the devil.

This view seems to erupt with renewed ferocity at the advent of every new form of popular music, especially popular music with a beat. It was espoused at the onset of punk in the 1970s, heavy metal in the '60s, rock in the '50s, and the big band sounds in the '30s. After jazz had invaded the mainstream of American music in the 1920s one critic in the New York Times went so far as to charge that "Jazz was borrowed from central Africa by a gang of wealthy international Bolshevists . . . [whose aim was] to strike at Christian civilizations throughout the world."[1] Whether we agree with the specifics of such remarks or not, we need to acknowledge that music is powerful and that its power can be used for good or for ill.

Like every other set of symbols we employ in worship, music inevitably communicates cultural and not simply religious messages. Music remembers the cultural context in which it was born; music is indelibly stamped with a cultural message which it perpetuates whether it is projected on a video screen, transmitted over radio waves or employed in the liturgy. The music we employ in our worship is not culture free. It carries implicit cultural messages that cannot be eliminated, though we might try to ignore them. For example, the dominance of European eighteenth-century harmonies in Christian worship music today implicitly communicates the superiority of a European eighteenth-century concept of God. Similarly, the elimination or complete camouflaging of dance rhythms in the people's music of the Christian West implicitly communicates that worship is not a dance, but something we do with feet planted firmly on the ground even though our minds might be reeling in the cloud of the unknowing. Thus, like every other symbol we employ in worship, music not only expresses our belief, it also shapes it.

Music shapes our faith, and it does so apart from the text. Many of us recognize that the texts we sing—the verbal images we employ—have an impact on our belief. The growing sensitivity to inclusive language in the United States is a clear testimony to this fact. What we sing does inevitably shape what we believe; but as musicians, we must also come to recognize that besides the words, the very music itself shapes our faith. And there are a number of ways in which this occurs.

The musical form, the very structure of a composition carries an ecclesiological message. The shape of the music says something about the shape of the community. Responsorial psalms, for example, communicate something very different from hymns. Responsorial forms embody dialogue; they say "you and me"; their very construction affirms the human and divine interchange which stands at the heart of Christian worship. Hymns, on the other hand, say "us" standing together, united in belief. Singing a hymn is a very different experience than singing a responsorial psalm, and it generates a very different self-consciousness. Hymn singing by its very nature is a more unitive experience, since the very form of the hymn does not allow for any participation other than that of the whole congregation. Hymns say "us."

Historically we know that hymns were essential to the reform of Martin Luther who was determined to tell Rome that the church was not the clergy but the assembly . . . that the church was not "you" or even "you-in-dialogue-with-us" but simply "us." Consequently Luther used an "us" form—the hymn—as an auditory metaphor for his vision of church, a picture in sound of his belief. That is why, to this day, Luther's hymns remain the best formulation of his theology.

Other elements of the music besides the musical forms also shape our faith, carrying implicit theological or ecclesiological messages. For example, music that requires the singer to have a two octave range, or even the more modest range of an eleventh, though it might be called congregational music, is not congregational. Our congregations seldom sing beyond the range of a ninth. Music that requires much more is beyond their competency and effectively excludes the vast majority of people in our assemblies.

But such music communicates much more than simple exclusion, for it implies that congregations really aren't expected to fulfill the roles given to them. If congregations are invited into music that they cannot perform—and everyone knows that they can't perform it—then why isn't it also true that congregations are invited into a way of life of which they are similarly incapable? Inviting people to sing music that they cannot or will not sing is effective preparation for a life in Christ which they cannot or will not live. Music shapes our faith.

Beyond the musical structures, however, there is another more illusive facet of our ministry that I believe is the single most powerful musical force we have for shaping the worship and belief of our assemblies, and that is the style of musical performance that we adopt in our ministry. One could stand here all evening and critique the quality of contemporary composition, the arrangements of these compositions, or their presentation by publishers. This is not, however, essentially a gathering of composers and publishers and the vast majority of us have little influence on them. What we do control, however, is how such music is performed in our churches. Therein is incredible potential for service or disservice to the liturgy.

Musical Leadership

The significance of the musical-liturgical performance became crystal clear to me in the fall of 1988, when I embarked upon a small field project in Chicago with Mary McGann, the director of liturgy and music at Loyola University. For a number of years Mary and I had been exploring various theories about congregational participation. One of those theories was that quality composition evoked quality participation. Since there was no data either to substantiate or disprove this hypothesis, we decided to test it in a three months study of six parishes in the Archdiocese of Chicago.

Very early in our study it became clear that the quality of composition was one of the least important factors in influencing the level of congregational participation. Much more important were things like the assembly's familiarity with the music and the relationship of the music to the rite. But of all the factors, the one

that consistently influenced the quality of congregational participation the most was the quality of the musical leadership. How
people led the music, had more influence on congregational participation than what music was sung.

In our study, the quality of the musical leadership was generally very good. That meant that very effective leadership often
engaged a community in the singing of sometimes quite mediocre music, and brought them to surprising levels of participation. Our study thus convinced me that the quality of the musical
leadership is at least as important as the quality of the liturgical
composition. My fear, however, is that both are struggling under
the influence of an entertainment model of worship which could
have devastating long-range effects on our common prayer.

In his brilliant and disturbing book *Amusing Ourselves to Death*,
Niel Postman claims that entertainment has become the most
common mode of public discourse in the United States today.[2]Postman suggests that politics and entertainment, education
and entertainment, news reporting and entertainment, and religion and entertainment are virtually indistinguishable. He be-
lieves this is true because entertainment, primarily as it is communicated through television, has become the primary mode of
public discourse in our society. Television has become our paradigm for communication: be that about world events, Hollywood
starlets, or divine truths. Postman summarizes:

> As the printing press did in an earlier time, television has achieved
> the power to define the form in which news must come, and it has
> also defined how we shall respond to it. In presenting news to us
> packaged as vaudeville, television induces other media to do the
> same, so that the total information environment begins to mirror
> television.[3]

The argument here is not completely new. In many respects it is
a recasting of Marshall McLuhan's previously quoted maxim,
"The medium is the message." If television is the medium, and if
television is essentially a medium for entertainment, then ultimately the message from television—no matter what the intended purpose of the show—will always be entertainment.

Postman contends that television has even forced religion in
this country to mirror entertainment. In support of this argument
he quotes the executive director of the National Religious Broad-
casters Association who sums up what he calls the unwritten law

of television preachers: "You can get your share of the audience only by offering [them] something they want." Postman comments:

> You will note, I am sure, that this is an unusual religious credo. There is no great religious leader—from the Buddha to Moses to Jesus to Mohammed to Luther—who offered people what they want. Only what they need. But television is not well suited to offering people what they need. It is "user friendly." It is too easy to turn off. It is at its most alluring when it speaks the language of dynamic visual imagery. It does not accommodate complex language or stringent demands. As a consequence, what is preached on television is not anything like the Sermon on the Mount. Religious programs are filled with good cheer. They celebrate affluence. Their featured players become celebrities. Though their messages are trivial, the shows have high ratings—or rather, because their messages are trivial, the shows have high ratings.[4]

I'm sure by now you are very glad that you are not a television evangelist, for they certainly are trivializing culture and religion. And what does all of this have to do with liturgy or music ministry? Only this: as Postman and others before him convincingly demonstrate, television is the most pervasive and powerful cultural influence in twentieth-century North America. It affects the way we think, the way we work, the way we relate and, I would contend, the way we believe. As liturgists and musicians, responsible for inviting people of various ages into the worship of the church, I also believe that a television mentality has influenced us: if for no other reason than we have to lead in prayer children who have been raised on Sesame Street and those cartoons now a major motion picture staring "Teenage Mutant Ninja Turtles"; we sacramentalize with adolescents nourished by "Whose the Boss" and "Teenage Mutant Ninja Turtles"; we eucharistize with young adults distracted by "LA Law" and "Teenage Mutant Ninja Turtles," we celebrate with parents informed by "Eyewitness News" and "Teenage Mutant Ninja Turtles" and we struggle to be faithful to senior citizens kept company by "Jeopardy" and . . . well, you get the picture.

And in the face of our competition . . . currently incarnate in the form of large, green, pizza eating reptiles we sometimes consciously or unconsciously attempt to fight entertainment techniques with entertainment techniques. It is my contention that entertainment techniques are increasingly apparent in the styles of our musical leadership. And to that extent, I suggest that we are trivializing divine truths or at least religious beliefs.

To be specific about how the entertainment model is influencing styles of our liturgical-musical leadership, I will first sketch some characteristics of such leadership in this vein, noting some of its consequences. Then I will offer a few directions for reversing this disturbing trend among liturgical musicians.

THREE CHARACTERISTICS OF THE ENTERTAINMENT SYNDROME

Artificial acoustics. One of the wonders of the electronic age is the invention and rapid improvement of amplification systems. This has been a great boon for preaching and sometimes for liturgical music as well. Increasingly, however, I find the acoustic environments of our worship spaces unfriendly to good liturgical music, and sympathetic to an entertainment style of leadership.

Consider a worship space with carpeting, acoustical tile, and padded pews. Devoid of any natural reverberation or resonance, the building includes an amplification system that is usually too powerful for the space. Singers crank up the gain, lean into the mikes, and funnel the amplified sounds of voices, piano, guitars, bass and synthesizer to a community standing on padded carpeting where it is impossible even to hear the person standing on your left or right when they sing. Your own voice, which sounds in isolation from the assembly, is often overpowered by the "music group". Sometimes this experience is exacerbated by a speaker system which gives the impression of disembodied music, that is, music that does not emanate from a sound source near the musicians, but spills out of those ubiquitous, invisible speaker grills in the ceiling.

Such an acoustic environment is artificial. It is akin to the sound system in a piano bar, where you are able to hear the performer no matter what the noise in the room or how far you are away from the piano. This environment creates an artificial sense of intimacy—but intimacy only with the musicians and not with other members of the assembly. Distant voices are amplified with clarion precision but, similar to a theater or concert hall, there is no reciprocal support for the voice of the assembly, which eventually learns to be quiet.

Music making as a visual event. It is no great revelation to note that music making is an event of the ear, not of the eye—an auditory, not a visual experience. Television, however, has mightily contributed to the transformation of music making from a sound to a sight event. To distinguish itself from radio, television developed ways to visualize the sound: to depict the performer and to match the musical display with a visual display. Sometimes that meant that the performer remained stationary, as in radio days, while the camera zoomed around taking close-ups, panning from the side, and intermingling shots of the audience. Eventually performers caught on and added the movements themselves. Elvis was a pioneer of visual music, so much so that during his first appearance on the Ed Sullivan show, camera shots of him were fixed from the waist up, preventing any images of his grinding pelvis from invading the living rooms of America. Today even the tamest of videos on MTV would make the people responsible for that decision turn over in their graves.

Superfluous gestures, costuming, distracting placement, nascent choreography and other staging techniques are increasingly apparent in our music ministries. One music director I know wore a sequined gown as her ministerial garb for a recent liturgy. There are certainly times when a cantor or a song leader needs to be visible to the community, but I do not believe that choirs, ensembles and instrumentalists need to be on a stage, offering visual display and rivaling the centrality of the action at the ambo, the altar, and in the midst of the assembly itself.

Showcase material. Every successful performer knows that it is important to select material that will most effectively showcase their talents. You select the key that flatters your range with a tessitura that shows off your voice, couched in an arrangement that complements your back-up singers. And unless you want to rest on your musical laurels, you are constantly in search of fresh and distinctive materials. Except for those few whose careers are built on nostalgia, repetition is musical suicide in the business.

My instinct is that similar showcasing principles are operative in the church today as we constantly search for fresh materials, for something unique and exciting that shows off our sound or shows off our taste. And this is true whether our search for new materials takes us into the latest releases or back into the six-teenth century, whether our group is a contemporary ensemble or a professional SATB choir. To the extent that the taste of the music group becomes the dominant criteria for selecting worship music, or to the extent that the need to find materials to showcase the group's talents becomes the dominant criterion for selecting music, then to that same extent have we moved out of liturgy and into the concert business.

Though other characteristics of the entertainment syndrome are invading our musical ministry, these three—artificial acous-tics, music making as a visual event, and showcase material—are sufficient to illustrate the point.

As to the effect of such techniques, remember that symbols not only express faith but also shape faith. And since symbols are cultural phenomena, they shape faith in terms of the culture that gave them birth. If we follow this line of thought to its logical conclusion, it is possible to suggest that musical-liturgical leader-ship cast in the entertainment mode produces what entertain-ment is meant to produce. It transforms an assembly into an audience, a congregation into spectators, and believers into li-turgical consumers. And, therefore, it transforms the commit-ment of an assembly, congregation and believers into the com-mitment of an audience, spectators and consumers.

Different types of performance evoke different types of com-mitment. A concert, for example, which focuses on the performer, evokes and perpetuates a commitment to the performer. Thus a concert by Cher or Michael Jackson is an exercise in adulation for Cher or Michael Jackson. The commitment is not so much to the event, or even to the music, as it is to the star, and people will go to unbelievable lengths to see such heroes. There are other types of performance that implicitly convey respect for a work of art apart from the performers, such as a Chechov play or a Beetho-ven symphony. These events, which often require considerable ensemble work and focus on the production, not simply the performer, do not evoke commitment to the star so much as they do to the art or the production. So people will often go to in-credible lengths to attend a production of "Les Miserables" or "The Magic Flute."

Employing an entertainment mode in worship produces simi-lar forms of commitment. In those places where the music revolves around a performer or performing group, the commitment that develops is one precisely to the performer or the group. In those places where the liturgy is staged as a great theater piece, the commitment is to the liturgy's effective production, its proper performance, and the maintenance of its quality no matter what changes in the ministry may occur.

It seems to me, however, that both of these fall short. Something has obviously gone awry when the focus of our worship is a star musician. But what may be more difficult for us to perceive is that something has also gone awry when the production of good liturgy is the main focus, for there is a critical difference between being committed to the production of good liturgy and being committed to the liturgy. The former is a commitment to a certain quality of performance, and the latter is a commitment to a certain quality of relationships and life in Christ. Many of our communities today seem committed to the performance, to "good liturgy," but that may be one of the empty accomplishments of the post-Vatican II liturgical movement if it doesn't also mean commitment to the mission implicit in liturgy. And people will never recognize much less accept the mission implicit in our worship if we give the impression that worship is an entertainment vehicle, and its most important result is enjoyment.

REVERSING THE TREND

So what do we do about that possibility? How do we stop the forward momentum of the entertainment model in American Roman Catholic worship and specifically in our own musical-liturgical leadership within that worship? I suggest that the first thing that we do is recognize that there is a problem. That in itself is a great step forward. It will also contribute to a clearer awareness during this phase of liturgical adaptation that adaptation does not mean wholesale acceptance of everything in a culture, but rather a critical appreciation of the interface between culture and worship, which by its very nature is countercultural.

Besides this general attentiveness let me make three other preliminary suggestions for stemming the entertainment tide in our worship and music ministry.

First of all, in terms of acoustics, introduce the standard of quality as outlined in Environment and Art in Catholic Worship.

As that document effectively defines it, quality means honesty and genuineness of materials.[5] For the musician this suggests genuineness in the acoustic environment; amplification on a human not olympic scale; volume and brilliance achieved by the training of the voice and not by playing with dials; and rejecting that false sense of intimacy where every breath is amplified as though you were on "General Hospital." Those who are building or renovating a worship space, work for such authentic acoustics. For the rest of us who may have little control over the spaces in which we worship, turn down the master volume and turn up the voices and instruments. It is more authentic.

Second, in order to counter the growing tendency to turn a musical into a visual one, try balancing the visibility of the music ministry with the visibility of the rest of the community. If you are in a space where the assembly can hardly see each other—banks of pews in basilica formation facing the sanctuary—be careful about giving the music ministry too much visual prominence. Think about placing most of them, especially the choir and instrumentalist, on the side with a more visible place for the cantor or song leader. Otherwise, a community that is confined by what could be considered theatrical seating will tend to assume the role of an audience and let you have the stage. In spaces where assembly members can see the faces of other worshipers, where the view is not limited to the backs of people's heads, allow the music ministry to assume a more visible position, but make sure it is one that has continuity with the assembly space and can never be construed as a stage.

Finally, in terms of counteracting the development of star material, think about creating a *Volk* standard in your worship, not a concert standard. Look for music in which the assembly will sound good, not just the musicians. That may mean that you evaluate music by means of the musical score and not the accompanying album or CD. Those are performance vehicles with fancy arrangements, overdubbing, and studio musicians creating a sound that is not reproducible in your assembly. So don't make it the standard for selecting music. Once the violins and synthesizers have been stripped away, what is left? You can't find that out from a recording. Labor over the score: it will improve your musicianship and allow you to select music that is congregationally singable and not just entertaining. Such labor will also force you to use your imagination in figuring out how you can turn the printed page into a musical event, and how you can do that over and over and over again.

A Formative Moment

When I began to prepare this presentation I started collecting stories, jokes, and parables about liturgy and show business. As I worked on this presentation, however, it dawned on me that to use them would be to adopt the very approach that I am now criticizing: for it would have meant turning this into an entertainment event, instead of what I hoped would be a moment of musical-liturgical formation. So I excised the funny material from these reflections. As I did that, I wondered to what extent I and others like me who have occasion to address groups in similar ways have been part of the problem. How many of us have approached liturgy as a business, or at least as a vocation with a business aspect that required just the right amount of staging, humor, and show biz know-how to fly? It is something we all need to change.

In his wonderful little book *All I Really Need to Know I Learned in Kindergarten,* Robert Fulghum wrote:

Wisdom is not at the top of the graduate-school mountain, but there in the sandpile at Sunday school. These are the things I learned:

share everything
play fair
don't hit people
put things back where you found them
clean up your mess
don't take things that aren't yours
say you're sorry when you hurt somebody
wash your hands before you eat
flush
warm cookies and milk are good for you
live a balanced life: learn some and think some
    and draw some and paint and sing and dance
    and play and work a little every day
take a nap every afternoon
when you go out into the world watch out for

traffic,
hold hands and stick together
be aware of wonder. Remember the little seed in
    the styrofoam cup: the roots go down and the
    plant goes up and nobody really knows how or
    why but we are all like that.
Goldfish and hamsters and white mice and even the
    little seed in the styrofoam cup—they all
    die. So do we
And remember the Dick-and-Jane books and the first
    word you learned—the biggest word of
    all—look
everything you need to know is in there somewhere.[6]

For those of us privileged to lead the song of the assembly, those of us privileged to sing the song of the Lamb, I would only add, look up: look up from your music, your director, your synthesizer, your organ console, your mixing board, and look into the faces of the people of God, look into the eyes of the assembly. Everything you need to know is in there somewhere. For that is the source of our ministry and the place of every return, made in the name of the Holy One risen in our midst, the Christ, who is Lord forever and ever.

Notes

1. "Says Jazz Threatens Christian Civilization," *New York Times* 16 (December 1934) 7.

2. Niel Postman, *Amusing Ourselves to Death: Public Discourse in the Age of Show Business* (New York: Penguin Books, 1985).

3. Ibid., 111.

4. Ibid., 121.

5. Bishops' Committee on the Liturgy, *Environment and Art in Catholic Worship* (Washington, D.C.: United States Catholic Conference, 1978) art. 20.

6. Robert Fulghum, *All I Really Need to Know I Learned in Kindergarten* (New York: Villard Books, 1988).

6

The Future of Church Music

Virgil C. Funk

Where is the future of church music? What a wonderful topic. It goes right along with, what's the future of the church? Obviously I have no crystal ball and most importantly the answer depends on what your viewpoint is, namely, how far do you stand away from the present to predict the future?

Church music is a lot like a sailboat sailing in the river or ocean. We could predict its future by examining its rigging, the solidness of its construction, and we could look at the aptitude of its sailors. But to really talk about its future course we would also have to look at what type of wind is in its sails and more importantly, is there a calm sea ahead or is there a hurricane coming? If a hurricane is coming, no amount of preparation on the part of the sailors, nor the quality of the craft, nor indeed the condition of the wind will make a difference. The sea will reach up and grab it.

Church music, like the sailboat, is dependent on a number of outside forces. In calm seas the outside forces do not play a significant role. It is the quality of the ship (the music) and the quality of sailors (the musicians) which will make a difference. But as we begin to make our examination, let us not forget that there are forces outside the field of church music that can and will influence its future in perhaps a more significant way than any factor within church music.

Several years ago, in 1982, John Naisbitt looked beyond particular aspects of our society, and published a book called *Mega-*

trends.[1] It was a great hit, and here is what he had to say about the country in 1982.

From:	*To:*
Industrial society	Information society
Forced technology	High/tech high/touch
National econony	World economy
Short term	Long term
Centralization	Decentralization
Institutional help	Self-help
Representative democracy	Participatory democracy
Hierarchies	Networking
North	South
Either/or	Multiple option

Notice the form of these trends. They are in a "from/to" order. Naisbitt's book was so successful and seemingly so accurate that eight years later he began (what I think will be a constant barrage from now until the year 2000) looking toward the year 2000.[2] This is what John Naisbitt recently said about the trends that will take us to the twentieth century.

1. The Booming Global Economy of 1990s
2. A Renaissance in the Arts
3. The Emergence of Free-Market Socialism
4. Global Lifestyles and Cultural Nationalism
5. The Privatization of the Welfare State
6. The Rise of the Pacific Rim
7. The Decade of Women in Leadership
8. The Religious Revival of the New Millennium
9. The Triumph of the Individual

Notice that he's changed his format away from "from/to." Naisbitt argues quite successfully, based on the increased sale of tickets, especially theater and opera, that there will be a renaissance in the arts (Trend 2). And, more interestingly, he argues that there will be a religious revival in the new millennium (Trend 8). He concludes his work:

We stand at the dawn of a new era. Before us is the most important decade in the history of civilization. A period of stunning technological innovation, unprecedented economic opportunity, surprising political reform, and great cultural rebirth. It is a decade like none that has come before because it will culminate in the millennium the year 2000.

When we think of the 21st century, we think of technology, space, travel, bio-technology, robots. But the face of the future is more complex than the technology we use to envision it. The most exciting breakthroughs of the 21st century will occur, not because of technology, but because of an expanding concept of what it means to be human.

With those hopeful ideas running around in our heads, let's turn our attention to our field of church music. I'd like to begin with an examination of the trends. Using Naisbitt's "from/to" model, what things are we letting go of and what things are we going toward? Here is my list.

From:	To:
Hymnody	Service music
Sing thematically	Sing liturgically
Sing everything, even poorly	Sing less, but well
Sacred treasure	Pastoral music
Praise only	Adoration/thanksgiving/ petition
Song leaders	Cantors
Choirs	More choirs
Parish musician	Musician/liturgist
Central leadership	Pastoral leadership

I am convinced that the major shift that will affect all of these trends is the move toward the pastoral model of being the church. This is summed up in the catch phrase "we are the church." It is a MEGA-megatrend, if I may say, that's expressed. And it controls our musical liturgy as the wind controls the direction of the sailboat. These points can be treated under four categories: what, how, who, and in what environment.

What Will We Be Singing?

In other words, just what will our repertoire sound like in the years ahead?

When I first came to the field of church music, I used to tell the story of an inner-city parish which was shifting from a black to a Hispanic community. A number of the wealthier blacks were moving from the community; the pastor had just been arrested for driving under the influence of alcohol; the parish advisory board had just notified the bishop that the school was going to be closing. In the midst of these disasters, the church musician was in his office trying to decide what was the proper song for next week. Should it be Marty Haugen or Richard Proulx?

I used that story to point out how musicians exaggerate the importance of repertoire in the face of social conditions, but that was fifteen years ago. Now with fifteen years of experience reflecting on church music, I am more and more convinced of just how dependent and service-oriented we church musicians are. We see our role as one of servants . . . not only do we serve our parish assembly, but we also serve the music (and the composer as well). It is as if we hide behind our music, let the music do the work, and we assist it. Although it is central and true that "good musicians make good music and bad musicians make bad music" and that "musicians are more important than repertoire," it is also true that the song we sing dramatically forms the assembly in worship.

This issue of the importance of the quality of the repertoire will continue to grow through the 1990s. We are more concerned about our repertoire now than we've ever been. At all of the past NPM conventions almost every major speaker has addressed the need for better craft in our compositions as well as in the performance of our repertoire.

Historically, we are moving away from "waves" of new music. We know that wave 1 in the late 1960s was Ray Repp and Lucien Deiss; wave 2 in the 1970s was the St. Louis Jesuits; wave 3 consisted of Haugen, Haas, Joncas; and perhaps wave 3 1/2 would be the St. Thomas More Centre with Chris Walker, Paul Inwood, and now Bernadette Farrell, and even the music of Taizé.

The question would be: What's next? I just don't know. What seems clear is that we will not be having a new wave of church music similar to Repp, the Jesuits, David Haas, and Marty Haugen. There will not be a time when one new composer sweeps across the country with a series of new songs. The day of the pop-star in liturgical music is thankfully over. The reasons are numerous: the climate has changed, our experimental time is coming to end; we have now developed bound hymnals, and we're settling in.

As we re-examine our congregational song, we will discover that hymnody has played an exaggerated role in the environment of Catholic liturgy. We will be moving toward a re-emphasis on singing the liturgy itself; not only the "Holy, Holy" and "Memorial Acclamation", but also the oldest part of the Roman Liturgy, the dialogue before the preface: "The Lord be with you" and "Lift up your hearts." We will be singing, on a regular basis, the penitential rite and the short response to the readings. In turn, that type of singing will move our liturgies away from a thematic liturgy to a recognition that we are celebrating a feast, and our musical selections will be more reflective of the liturgical feasts. This will help us to resist the temptation to select the hymn we know or the "sing anything as long as they can sing it" approach to a more critical awareness that the liturgical/musical judgments (expressed in the Bishops' document Music in Catholic Worship) must be applied more seriously and strenuously.

In summary then, *what* we will be singing will be less hymns and more service music.

How Will We Sing?

We now move to our second area of concern, how we sing or the style of singing. These are listed in my trends 4, 5, and 6. While all musicians realize that music is a performance art, not every pastor does. How the music is performed makes all the difference in the quality of the music. Good music, performed poorly, can certainly be a disaster. Mediocre music, performed with life, can lift the spirit in a way that surprises both musician and music maker. The following principles regarding how the music is performed, I feel, will come into play more and more in church music.

We will move from "sing everything" to "sing a few things well." However, I do not think that every parish will move in this direction. To go back to our master image of church music being like a sailboat, the more accurate picture is that church music is like a number of sailboats: some of them are sleek schooners with high-class captains who have spent a lot of money on their boats, and some are very small, one-person, sailboats. All of them are affected by the wind, all of them are affected by the water, but quite frankly, not all of them can do the same thing. Not all of them can tack in the same breeze at the same speed, not all of them can ride the same size waves.

The same is true of music programs in diverse parishes. In an issue of *Pastoral Music*,[3] Bob Batastini described an occasion when the people were told that they would now sing their gathering song. The organ played an introduction, the first verse was sung by nine members of the congregation, the second verse was sung by five members of the congregation, and the priest then said: "Now that we have completed our song of gathering, let us begin 'In the name of the Father, and the Son, and of the Holy Spirit'."

Bob called this "pretend music." It wasn't really a gathering song at all. Perhaps when the priest ad-libbed the liturgical text "Let us *begin*. . . In the name of the Father, and the Son, and the Holy Spirit," he told a truth that's more profound than he or we care to admit, namely, that the opening act of gathering through music didn't work.

Music performs a function in liturgy. The opening song is to gather the assembly. If the act of gathering does not occur through music, then we have "pretend music." As church musicians come to consciousness about this reality, they will make the choice of singing fewer things well, rather than simply having a list of music which is to be sung every Sunday regardless of whether its performing its liturgical function or not. When a congregation hears the beauty of its own song, it is enamored of that sound and will try and repeat it. Sing "Amazing Grace" and watch what happens when you reach "When I've been there ten-thousand years." We all know the effect of a song sung well in motivating a congregation to sing. The old cliché "nothing succeeds like success" is especially true of music. We musicians, for the future, must concentrate on having successes with our congregational song. This will mean for many of our parishes that we will stop trying to sing everything . . . and poorly so . . . and start concentrating on singing a few things well.

We will move from sacred treasure to pastoral music. An often quoted paragraph from the Second Vatican Council says: "The treasure of sacred music is to be preserved and fostered with great care." This sacred treasure (that is, polyphony, formal music) is then qualified: "Bishops and pastors must be at pains to ensure that whenever the sacred action is to be celebrated with song, the whole body of faithful must be able to contribute that act of participation which is rightly theirs." (Constitution on the Sacred Liturgy, no. 114) This qualification gave rise to the development of music which is sung by the congregation. Most of us are aware of the development that took place in the United States, music that was primarily composed for and performed by the ensemble groups of the 1960s and which led to a revolution in understanding congregational song in the United States. Although a similar revolution did not take place on a wide scale in Germany, France, or Italy, the term "sacred treasure" has become synonymous with formal music and the term "pastoral" has been identified with the shift to congregation song. I believe that this trend will continue in the future and the quality of pastoral music will increase, but still it will be governed by the liturgical, pastoral, and important musical quality controls that were laid down by the 1968 Roman Instruction on Sacred Music and reiterated in Music and Catholic Worship by the U.S. bishops.

The third trend will be to move from praise music to adoration, thanksgiving/praise, and supplication. One of the present characteristics of our music is to sing music which sounds alike. Somehow we have gotten into a rut in thinking that all of our music must be praise-oriented. When we look at the structure of the Roman Mass, we find that moments of praise are actually very limited. Although thanksgiving is central to the act of worship, thanksgiving can be expressed in more forms than that of praise; in addition, our liturgical rite calls for moments of adoration and supplication.

The assembly is asked to stand before God begging, entreating, supplicating for mercy. The disposition of a grieving creature seeking communication and favors from an almighty and loving God is not presently reflected in our liturgical music. The "Lord, Have Mercy", the prayer of the faithful, and even the fraction rite with its litanic "Lamb of God" are all intended to be moments of intercession, entreating, the petitioning of children before their all-loving Father. Our liturgical music at these moments is remarkably similar to the music that we sing at the other moments of the rite. "Holy God, Holy Mighty One, Holy Immortal . . . Have mercy on us."

Adoration is often the disposition which is triggered following the readings in the responsorial psalm, and we end up reducing this text to a momment of joyous festivity.

Readers of *Pastoral Music* will remember the wonderful article of Joseph Gelineau entitled "Litany as Supplication"[4] where he created metaphors for how our music should sound: the act of praise is like climbing to a mountaintop where once you have reached the top there is nowhere else to go. Musically, it is like the last Alleluia of the "Hallelujah Chorus." You don't need to sing another one.

The act of adoration is like a deep wave in the ocean reflecting back on itself, giving time for internal reflection; the act of supplication is like the ocean striking the beach, having an intense impact and then a release . . . repeating over and over again the intense action of the wave churning up the sand then releasing it upon the beach. When we sing *ab omne malo, te rogamus audi nos; ab omne peccato, te rogamus audi nos*, we can feel the movement of petitioning and release.

Who Will Sing?

In addition to the development of our repertoire (the what) and our style (the how), there will also be the development of our musicians (the who). To repeat: "Good musicians make good music, bad musicians make bad music." It's that simple. We need musicians who can play and sing our repertoire. I believe we have a wide range of very effective repertoire that we have not yet adequately used—because our musicians cannot play it well.

The trends here are really frightening. If you have read Alan Bloom's chapter on music in *The Closing of the American Mind* (and I recommend that you do), you will realize just how frightening things might be. He maintains that the "Walkman" which has become such a powerful commercial force for the college-age students is dominating the intellectual life of our community. He says that college-age students long for the time when they can leave the intellectual world and move to an art form directed exclusively to children.

> Picture a thirteen-year-old boy sitting in a living room of his family home doing his math assignment or while wearing his walkman headphone or watching MTV. He enjoys the liberties hard won over centuries by the alliance of philosophic genius and political heroism, consecrated by the blood of martyrs; he is provided with comfort and leisure by the most productive economy ever known to humankind; science has penetrated the secrets of nature in order to provide him with the marvelous, lifelike electronic sound and image reproduction he is enjoying. And in what does progress culminate? A teenage child whose body thrives with orgasmic rhythms, whose feelings are made articulate in hymns to the joys of onanism or the killing of parents.
>
> The result is nothing less than parents' loss of control over their children's moral education at a time when no one else is seriously concerned with it. My concern here is not with the moral effect of this music, whether it leads to sex, violence, or drugs, the issue here is its effect on education and I believe it ruins the imagination of young people and makes it very difficult for them to have a passionate relationship to the art and thought that are the substance of liberal education.[5]

Alan Bloom's analysis goes along with our experience that music's role is changing in modern times. We no longer sing the national anthem at a baseball game. Families no longer gather around the piano. People no longer gather in our drinking establishments for community sings.

Music effects the music makers. The American Guild of Organists points to fewer organists; music schools point to fewer students; and we point to fewer interested in music making.

Using our master metaphor of the sailboat, we can now look at the crew and the captain, namely the musicians.

The Song Leader. The song leader of ten years ago has become the psalmist or cantor, no longer with the primary responsibility of encouraging congregational song through hand gesture and leadership. The psalmist is a liturgical minister within the Roman Liturgy. And make no mistake about it, the General Instruction of the Roman Missal calls for a cantor to serve as an animator or facilitator of the dynamic of the rite, but the role (developed in America) of a gesticulating song leader is coming to an end.

Choirs. A very clear trend is that there is a movement toward choirs. Certainly any number of choirs faced an identity crisis in the years immediately following Vatican II. The period of turmoil is now over. Choirs are once again flourishing. As is evident from the various NPM conventions, musicians are showing a tremendous interest in the role and function of choirs.

Director of the Ministries of Music. Professionally there is no question that a shift is going on in our field. Immediately following the council, a number of people who were parish organists became "the parish musicians." The National Association of Pastoral Musicians encouraged the pastoral musician to name him- or herself more accurately and suggested that the primary role for a church musician would be better named the Director of the Ministries of Music. This title reflects the multiple roles in worship: the congregation, the presider, the accompanist, the cantor, etc. and that all of these (when making music) are under the Director of the Ministries of Music. But what is also happening in our field is that a number of priests are asking the musician to assume leadership in liturgy. As a result, those musicians who are double-degreed or have the capicity to be both musician and liturgist are the ones who are attracting the highest salaries and are being recognized as the most competent. We are definitely getting into the era of the musician as liturgist.

In What Environment?

So much for looking at the sailboats in the bay and the people who are sailing them. Perhaps we now need to step back and look at the condition of the water and the wind.

The greatest, overarching, influence on church music is the relationship between the clergy and the musician. In our times we have experienced a tremendous shift in the power base, from the clergy to the assembly. It is captured in the phrase, "We are the church." The making of church music in every parish is dependent on the state of the shift. Even where this shift has been resisted, it exercises a new and pervasive influence on a parish's liturgical life.

The reality of what it means to be church today and tomorrow will not emanate from Rome, but will emerge from our shared reflections on our experiences as church in various cultural settings. The experience many of us are now having with the hierarchy, the present attempt to recall all power to the Curia and to issue decrees from that central authority, will fail precisely because such decrees will be less and less applicable to our everyday lived experience.

Second, music is influence by the theology of the times and by the age's master image of God. The nineteenth-century image of "God-in-his-Heaven-and-all-is-right-with-the-world" produced music that was magnificent and baroque and romantic; the twentieth century has stressed the God of Genesis—made in the image and likeness—with whom we have a personal relationship, and our music reflects it.

The Jacob and Esau story is still true. Jacob steals his brother's birthright and blessing and flees lest Esau kill him. In the dark of night, utterly exhausted from flight, he falls asleep on the desert's barren landscape where he dreams of a ladder stretching from heaven to earth and angels going up and down. Awakening in this apparently god-forsaken terrain, he utters what is perhaps the most sublime line in the whole Bible, "Surely God is in this place and I did not know it." Therein lies our challenge. In today's churches, people see reflected not their dreams, but their nightmares of lonely days and nights that have become the reality of their lives. They wake up and unlike Jacob say, "Maybe God is in this place, but you'd never know it." We need to transform the barren landscape of our communal lives into real communities of total responsibility. There, in the intimacy of mutual care, we will know the reality of God. Let people rise from their worship then, and looking into each other's eyes say as Jacob did, or maybe even better: "Surely God is in this place and we know it all along".[6]

This pastoral shift leads to singing repertoire dominated by images and theology of our times. It excludes poorly crafted texts . . . because the assembly will ultimately reject them. The group of composers will remain small but the nature of what they do changes. Look at Proulx and Kreutz taking old forms and evolving new musical forms from them. Eclectic celebrations will in-

crease due to the pastoral evolution. We are no longer a Eu-
ropean-based church; the great majority of Roman Catholics by
the year 2000 will live outside the European-North American
sphere. We are in Africa, Latin America, and Asia. Their cultures,
while influenced by those of Europe and the United States, are
radically different from our own, and the life of their churches
more and more reflects that difference. One liturgical example:
it's impossible to celebrate the officially approved Zaire Rite for
the eucharist without dancing parts of it—and that means the
presider as well as the congregation. Here in the United States,
it will mean that we'll have to attend to the various cultures
labeled "Hispanic." This means not only a new musical repertoire, but also various changes in the way we worship to reflect
the rhythms and emphasis of those cultures. That change may
also lead to a kind of culturally mixed liturgy, part in English,
part in Spanish, and an appropriate mixed musical repertoire as
well.

Third, because of the declining number of priests, we will
move away from what Aidan Kavanagh has identified as our
reduction of symbols to the eucharist. The absence of a priest
presider will mean that a parish cannot celebrate the eucharist
each time it celebrates baptisms, marriages, and funerals. Some
deacons (but mostly lay presiders) can and will lead those celebrations, but they will probably be events that do not include
even communion from the reserved sacrament. How will we
define eucharist? And will the eucharist continue to define us?
The other rites (in addition to the eucharist) that require the
presence of an ordained minister, confirmation, penance, and the
anointing of the sick, will obviously be less available than at the
present. What will we as church do about that? Some of these
rites, for example, the anointing of the sick and perhaps some
aspects of sacramental penance, may be transferred to lay ministers (as they have been in the past).

All these sacramental celebrations will require a music minister. It's hard for us to imagine a festive celebration of, let us say,
a wedding, without music. The need people have for music, even
at a funeral, is testified to by the growth of the resurrection choirs
in this country. The music more and more will be pastoral, namely, subject to the demands of the community participating in the

event. More and more of it may be service music, music that is part of the rite and proper to the rite, like the final commendation at the funeral, not thematic hymnody that is tacked on at convenient points. And yet it is true that the revised order of Christian funerals does identify some hymns that have become standard parts of American Catholic funerals. But the move toward service music may also signal the demise of the hardback hymnal being a participation aid, as such large collections of hymnody become less necessary and useful.

As this pastoral shift takes place, the craft of the musical leader will increase, less often in response to "the-pastor-asked-me-to-be-the-musician," but more due to the demands of the music itself. The higher percentage of working musicians who are educated will in turn influence the music, namely, they will effect what arrangements are created. If you don't have saxophone players, you won't have music written for saxophone, and so on.

Due to the information explosion, more people know what's going on in the next parish. Odious comparisons between good music, strong repertoire, and lively assembly singing to poor music, weak repertoire, and dead communities will force a change quicker than any theory. These pastoral shifts may be a fifty- to a hundred-year trend and not an immediate one.

What will happen in the clerical world will still dominate. If we have a married priesthood, if we have women as priests, there will be a major trend outside the field of music that's going to influence us, but the musician still has to take on the hard responsibility for adapting to pastoral reality. In the next ten to thirty years we'll know what's appropriate for church and what's not. I think it's getting clearer.

The primary of the pipe organ in the nineteenth century will not withstand the technological development. It will remain a delight for us specialists; but it's going to decrease—not just because of cost, but also the architecture for pastoral liturgy just doesn't allow for the space for a full pipe organ. All buildings will indeed have technology, but not all will have sound buildings for organs.

I don't think anyone doubts that the strong wind of the Second Vatican Council that was blowing in the sails of church music has lessened in the last five years. Our musical and liturgical boats are definitely not sailing at the speed they used to. It's fair to say that a number of squalls and storms have affected our work. The fundamental shift to the pastoral has been reinforced by developments in communication theory. But make no doubt about it, we musicians are not shipwrecked. We are alive and sailing under full sail.

In conclusion, that's the way I see things shaping up. It's generally a hopeful picture because I have great hope for the church's future. I believe that in the next twenty or thirty years we will see a great shifting going on. It is gradually becoming clear that certain things are appropriate for us do and be as a church, whereas others are not, at least at this time in our history. We will learn to select not only from historical models of what it means to be church, but also to select from the culture what is of value and what is not. Earlier I referred to cultural models like car stereos and boomboxes to suggest that music is for listening, not for doing. Music for worship is for doing, not primarily for listening, as we know so well. So we need to encourage congregational singing as we have been doing for decades and to oppose the cultural trend that will have us listen silently while others perform.

If you ever visit Washington, D.C., go to the Kennedy Center for the Performing Arts. Stand on the porch overlooking the Potomac. Look at the sailboats going in all directions, just as our parishes are. Imagine the turbulent sea, the strong or light wind, and indeed the impending hurricane. But as you turn around and face the building, you will see the wonderful quotes of John F. Kennedy which are etched on the wall of the magnificent building. Allow me to conclude with a paraphrase of his wonderful hope for our country as an expression of my hope for the future of church music.

I look forward to a church which will reward achievement in the arts as we reward achievement in catechesis or priesthood. I look forward to a church which will steadily raise the standards of artistic accomplishment and which will steadily enlarge cultural opportunities for all of our members. And I look forward to a church which commands respect throughout the world not only for its size but for its commitments to gospel values.

* * * * * *

The church cannot afford to be materially rich and spiritually poor.

* * * * * *

I am certain that after the dust of centuries has passed over our churches, we too will be remembered not for liturgical celebrations or musical performances, but for our contribution to the human spirit.

* * * * * *

There is a connection, hard to explain logically but easy to feel, between achievements in public life and progress in worship. The age of Augustus was also the age of Jesus. The age of Justinian the Great was also the age of Roman chant. The age of Charlemagne was also the age of Alcuin. The age of John Kennedy was also the age of Pope John XXIII. And the new era of the church music which is so changing our public understanding of God will bring a new frontier of faith.

Notes

1. John Naisbitt, *Megatrends: Ten New Directions Transforming Our Lives* (New York: Warner Books, 1982).

2. John Naisbitt with Patricia Aburdene, *Megatrends 2000: Ten New Directions for the 1990's* (New York: Morrow, 1990).

3. Robert Batastini, "Our People Just Don't Like to Sing," *Pastoral Music* 2:1 (October–November 1977) 54.

4. Joseph Gelineau, "Litany as Supplication," *Pastoral Music* 12:6 (August–September 1988) 21–22.

5. Alan Bloom, *The Closing of the American Mind* (New York: Simon & Schuster, 1987) 75.

6. Lawrence A. Hoffman, *The Art of Public Prayer: Not for Clergy Only* (Washington, D.C.: The Pastoral Press, 1988) 178.

Contributors

Mary Collins, O.S.B. is on the faculty of The Catholic University of America in Washington, DC. Among her many publications are *Worship: From Renewal to Practice* (The Pastoral Press, 1987) and *Called to Prayer: Liturgical Spirituality Today* (The Liturgical Press, 1986).

Eugenio Costa, S.J. teaches at the Centro Teologico in Turin, Italy, and is a member of the Praesidium of *Universa Laus*.

Edward Foley, Capuchin, chairs the Word and Worship Department at the Catholic Theological Union in Chicago. He is the editor of the "American Essays in Liturgy" series available from The Liturgical Press.

Virgil C. Funk is the President of The National Association of Pastoral Musicians and has edited many publications for The Pastoral Press.

Lawrence A. Hoffman is professor of liturgy at Hebrew Union College-Jewish Institute of Religion in New York. He is the author of *The Art of Public Prayer: Not for Clergy Only* (The Pastoral Press, 1989) and coeditor of *The Changing Face of Christian and Jewish Worship in North America* (University of Notre Dame Press, 1991).

David N. Power, O.M.I. is a faculty member at The Catholic University of America, Washington, DC. Among his numerous books are *Unsearchable Riches: The Symbolic Nature of Liturgy* (Pueblo Publishing Co., 1984) and *Worship: Culture and Theology* (The Pastoral Press, 1991).